BIO-DYNAMIC
GARDENING

By the same author
STUDYING THE AGRICULTURAL COURSE

BIO-DYNAMIC GARDENING

John Soper

Revised and enlarged by
B. Saunders-Davies and K. Castelliz

SOUVENIR PRESS

First published 1983 by the Bio-Dynamic Agricultural Association
Copyright © 1983 by John Soper
This edition copyright © 1996 by the Bio-Dynamic Agricultural Association

The right of John Soper to be identified as author of this work
has been asserted by him in accordance with the Copyright,
Designs and Patents Act 1988.

The edition first published 1996 by
Souvenir Press Limited, 43 Great Russell Street,
London WC1B 3PD
and simultaneously in Canada

Reprinted in 2002

ISBN 0 285 63279 5

Typeset in Great Britain by
Rowland Phototypesetting Limited, Bury St Edmunds, Suffolk
Printed in Great Britain by
The Guernsey Press Co. Limited, Guernsey, Channel Islands

Contents

Foreword

John Soper met the Bio-Dynamic work before the War and has remained faithful to it ever since. In East Africa, while in the Colonial Agricultural Service, he broadcast gardening talks both in English and Swahili, and was chairman of the Dar-es-Salaam horticultural society. In his work in the Colonial Service he always took a broad view, advocating a healthy organic way. He has often told me that much that was done in those days has now sadly disappeared. Wherever he lived he always had a garden. After his retirement he took up work for the Bio-Dynamic Agricultural Association.

This book is the fruit of all those years. It is that excellent kind of book—a man's own experience. It will, I hope and believe, be valued by those interested in Bio-Dynamic gardens and their background for many years to come.

David Clement
formerly Chairman,
Bio-Dynamic Agricultural Association

Foreword to the Second Edition

When a second edition of this book was proposed, it was suggested that more should be added on cosmic influences and herbs as there is a growing public interest in these subjects. We have therefore enlarged the descriptions of the bio-dynamic preparations and their effects, as this surely adds much interest and understanding when using them.

Taking account of cosmic influences is one of the main differences between bio-dynamic and organic methods. The earth is on the downward path of dying and is being so abused that it needs more positive help than merely avoiding the use of chemical fertilisers and herbicides and reverting to older, traditional methods. These are good as far as they go, but in order to enliven the declining forces in nature, an intelligent use of the bio-dynamic preparations brings new possibilities to farmers and gardeners.

We have also added sections on weeds and insect and animal pests. These are more fully treated in Maria Thun's publications to which we have referred.

The book remains substantially as John Soper wrote it, but additions have been made to the text to bring in new information, and completely new chapters are clearly attributed, such as that on herbs. The list of recommended varieties of fruit and vegetables has been revised and brought up to date by the bio-dynamic market gardener Jean Cormack and others, as some of John Soper's suggestions are no longer available. The added varieties have been marked with an asterisk as a guide to those familiar with the previous edition.

A few comments have been added to an enlarged book list to assist readers in their selection, and addresses have been provided of those publishers whose books are not easily obtainable through the normal retail outlets.

B. Saunders-Davies
1996

Acknowledgements

We would like to thank the following for their help in preparing the revised edition of this book:

Jean Cormack for her advice on varieties of fruits and vegetables suitable for bio-dynamic techniques;
Tabitha Parsons for her drawings of the preparation plants;
James Anderson for contributing photographs to illustrate bio-dynamic gardening in practice.

Preface

In an address to those attending his course of lectures on agriculture Rudolf Steiner explained that he was giving them a kind of alphabet, and that it would be up to each of them to make the letters into words which would apply to their own particular conditions of soil, climate, etc. He emphasised that he was speaking from his personal experience on small peasant farms, and he did not mention gardens at all. Moreover when he spoke of seasons he referred specifically to those which prevail in a continental climate. Dr E. Pfeiffer, Erica Riese, Maria Thun and others have made many useful words out of the new alphabet, words applicable to gardens, but again under continental conditions. But the insular climate and many of the soil types of Great Britain are not quite the same as those on the continents of Europe and North America, nor have we been fortunate enough to have had anything approaching a research station with workers devoted to the making of British words. Nevertheless a certain amount of scattered experience has been gathered by a number of gardeners over the years since the Agriculture Course was first brought over to Britain in the early 1930s, and many people feel that these threads need to be brought together. This I have now tried to do.

In writing the book I have had in mind especially those who may be coming to gardening for the first time and also those more experienced gardeners who are coming to bio-dynamics for the first time. The chapters dealing with individual crops do not purport to be a complete guide in every detail; I have concentrated more on aspects which, from personal experience, may be at variance with the advice given in some standard text books. I have also described many of the commoner troubles which may arise in even the most harmonious gardens from time to time, and have made suggestions for preventing them or for dealing with them if they do occur. A great deal more remains to be learned, so in the final chapter I have collected several instances where some preliminary observations seem to be worth following up; other possible lines of work will no doubt occur to readers. In the present circumstances of the Bio-Dynamic Agricultural Association in Britain advances in understanding basic principles and in devising techniques for applying them can only be made by co-operative effort. Readers are therefore invited to send particulars of any significant observations and trials to the Secretary of the Association or to the Editor of *Star and Furrow*.

This book could not have been written without the assistance of the late George Corrin, the Association's Consultant. Several important passages in the text are slightly paraphrased extracts from articles which he wrote, and he put his wide experience unstintingly at my disposal throughout. To him we all owe a deep debt of thanks.

John Soper
Clent
June 1982

CHAPTER 1

Introducing Bio-Dynamics

More and more people today are becoming convinced in their hearts that the world which we see and hear around us is not the only one; behind it and beyond the range of our senses there must be other worlds which underlie, inform, permeate and organise all our natural surroundings. The truth of this inner feeling is supported by the experiences of seers throughout the ages and in particular more recently by the revelations of Rudolf Steiner. Such an inner realisation is stronger and more far-reaching than the instinctive reaction of those who appreciate the damage being done to the earth by technology both in agriculture and industry, but who are trying to solve the problem simply by a return to more natural methods; they are still thinking with an 'onlooker' substance-bound consciousness. The former outlook prompts one to begin studying nature and life in terms of processes, functions and dynamic qualities rather than in terms of mere matter. And so one comes to see that in nature cosmic factors have to be taken into consideration, and that Spirit is the original creator of matter, penetrating into its essential being and all its activities. Our plants and animals come to be seen as organisms manifesting themselves in their own right, not subject merely to chemical and physical laws, but also to all the unseen forces and influences streaming out from the earth and in from the universe.

It then has to be acknowledged that we ourselves, in our physical bodies, are part and parcel of this whole. We are not just onlookers manipulating nature to suit our personal ends.

The food which we eat, the water we drink, the air we breathe all bind us inseparably to the biosphere; to work effectively in this milieu we have to learn to think as participants. This is not easy, but there are several ways which can help towards this new approach to nature. First and foremost it is beneficial to start developing a sense of wonder, humility and reverence. We can begin to experience within ourselves the rhythm of the seasons and their varying moods. We can try to sharpen our powers of perception, especially by noting day by day the changes in a familiar scene—the clouds, the play of the light, the growth of selected plants, and so on. Then one can try to experience the development of the annual plant by holding a viable seed in one's hand and watching it in imagination germinate, produce roots and leaves, flower, set seed and die. All this is a gradual process and many may not attain full transformation in a lifetime; but regular practice soon creates the frame of mind for appreciating and applying bio-dynamic methods.

One of the fundamental ideas underlying the bio-dynamic approach is that this earth of ours is a living organism in its own right. The astronauts experienced this and expressed their feelings in general terms, but it can also be seen in terms of the usually accepted functions of a living creature. The idea is not new; it is as old as the human race itself, but it has fallen into disrepute in this materialistic age. A famous alchemist, Basilius Valentinus, expressed it thus:

> The earth is not a dead body, but is inhabited by a spirit that is its life and soul. All created things, minerals included, draw their strength from the earth spirit. This spirit is life, it is nourished by the stars and it gives nourishment to all the living things it shelters in its womb. Through the earth spirit received from on high, the earth hatches the minerals in her womb as the mother her unborn child.

The earth breathes, it has a circulatory system, it has a pulse, it is sensitive and it has a skin. It breathes out during the morning hours, in during the afternoon and rests during the night. Its circulatory system is provided by the water cycle as it evaporates from oceans and lakes, returns as rain and flows back to the seas through river systems and underground streams. Like blood in an animal or sap in a plant, substances are brought in solution to where they are needed and waste products are carried away for recycling. The changing seasons act as a kind of pulse; during spring and summer in the northern hemisphere there is an outpouring, an expansive process, while at the same time in the southern hemisphere the contractive forces of autumn and winter are operating; and then the roles are reversed. This gigantic pulse beat is discernible right down (or up) to the equator, and there are only very few places which do not come under its influence in one way or another. E. and L. Kolisko demonstrated this rhythm very convincingly by a series of experiments in which various substances in solution were put to crystallise out at different depths beneath the soil; the contracting crystallising forces rose to a peak in January-February, and faded quite markedly in June-July. Then it does not need much imagination to see the soil/plant complex of the earth as a skin; everybody will have noticed how rapidly wounds caused by cuttings or landslides are healed by a plant covering. This complex also acts as a sense organ, telling the earth what is coming in from the cosmos, and by the nature of the vegetation telling the cosmos what is going on at any particular place on the earth's face.

In all garden work it is helpful to try to plan one's tasks in accordance with the daily expansion/contraction rhythm of the earth. Weather conditions and other factors may make this impossible on various occasions, but nevertheless as an acquired habit it will lead towards a closer and more rewarding relationship with the plant world. For example, the outpouring morning period is the best time for harvesting leaf vegetables and flowers, especially any that are to be dried for herbal purposes: at this time also seedlings and other plants ready to be transplanted can be lifted and put away till evening in a cool shady place. Afternoon and evening are better for sowing seeds, planting out transplants and for harvesting roots.

Another feature of the natural world which was recognised by people of old but is now generally disregarded is a force which can broadly be called 'levity'. It has a kind of outward-pulling suctional effect, an expanding influence, but in no way related to a reduction of physical pressure. The concept was dropped soon after the apple fell on Newton's head, and a gravity-based science began to be developed. It is strange that at that time nobody appears to have questioned the peculiar fact that this new gravity was the only quality operating in the world which did not have a polar opposite—hot and cold, dry and moist, positive and negative electricity, and so on. Gravity is point-centred, contractive, pulling everything downwards; levity has its 'centre' in the periphery of the universe; it is expansive, drawing everything outwards. Wherever there is life of any kind we find contraction/expansion processes at work, creating rhythmic pulses as first one and then the other preponderates; we find these rhythms in an almost infinite number of forms varying from seconds to years, from milligrams to tonnes. The recognition of this fundamental and universal polarity provides the basis for much of bio-dynamic thought and practice.

Yet another factor of major importance to the understanding of bio-dynamic practices is the idea that the material substances in a living organism are not in the same condition as similar substances in a chemical laboratory. In the former case the substances (chemical elements) are in a continual flux: some new ones come in, some old ones are deposited or excreted—there is no beginning and no end other than conception (or fertilisation) and death. In the latter case, when certain substances are mixed together, often in aqueous solution, a chemical reaction takes place more or less quickly and that is the end of it. In the first case it is as if the elements partake in the life of their host and are themselves alive; in the second case they are corpses. Active functions are manifested as against mere properties. It has already been postulated that matter derives from spirit; here is an example where on the one hand spirit is still active while on the other hand it has finished its work. Each chemical element has its own special part to play in a living complex; it is then in what E. Lehrs called its 'young' or 'alert' state. In practice, by careful methods of composting, the attempt is made to retain as much as possible of this 'alertness' for enlivening the soil and providing the future plants with active nutrients. If we try to stimulate a plant by adding soluble dead substances to the soil, it will have to expend some of its own life energy in raising such substances from the inert to the alert state, and this will have a weakening effect.

In the Agriculture Course Rudolf Steiner paints the ideal picture of a farm as a self-contained individual organism capable of producing out of its own resources and those of the cosmos a surplus for the benefit of mankind. The various features of a farm, the livestock, meadows, arable land, hedges, streams, ponds, trees, orchards, wild life, and even the plants on the borders of fields, blend together to form a harmonious product-ive whole. It is not so easy to apply this concept of self-containedness to a garden. Nevertheless, most gardens can have an individuality of their own which will be emphasised or diminished according to the diversity of its features, their bal-ance and the way in which they are nourished. The bio-dynamic gardener therefore aims to introduce a wide variety of plants whose natures will work together to form a radiant health-giving whole. Like it or not, a garden will to a certain extent also be a reflection of the gardener himself, for he is part of it. No two gardens are exactly the same. Each one is made up of its own soil type, aspect, climate, slope and general surroundings, and these in turn are worked on and modified by the owner with his own attitudes and purposes. Together all these factors build up a kind of organism with its own dim life, in harmony or conflict with the biosphere as the case may be. It is therefore quite impossible to lay down hard and fast rules to suit every occasion: what is a right practice in one case could be disastrous in another. So in this book we shall be concerned with general principles; it will be up to the reader to adapt them to his own particular circumstances.

CHAPTER 2
Cosmic Influences

It is all too easy to speak glibly about cosmic influences, Spirit and so forth, but as mere words they do not get us very far unless we struggle to form clear and ever clearer mental pictures about the nature of the forces and entities which are operating. In olden times under the guidance of the priest kings, many of the events on earth, its living creatures and even its substances were clairvoyantly seen to be reflections of celestial bodies and their movements. This living knowledge slowly degenerated into superstition, witchcraft and popular astrology, but traces of the genuine tradition were still to be found in peasants' calendars and among primitive peoples up to the middle of this century. Now the latter beliefs are almost completely lost; but on the other hand there is a strongly growing interest not so much in retrieving the past but more towards rediscovering its basis with a more direct consciousness. The following account describes the background and some of the facts which have been brought to light.

The Zodiac

The zodiac is the ring of twelve constellations against which the sun, as seen from the earth, appears to move during the course of the year, and the moon every month. They were recognised and depicted by initiates and seers thousands of years ago when men felt a much closer relationship to the universe than is the case today. The actual constellations are of varying sizes, and each has its own distinctive quality which is imparted particularly to sun and moon when they stand in front of them. One must therefore look for subtle qualitative differences in sunlight and moonlight during the annual and monthly courses of these bodies. The nature of these differences is traditionally connected with the four elements—earth, water, air/light and fire, represented in the plant by root, leaf, flower and fruit respectively.

In speaking about the zodiac there is often some confusion over the use of the terms 'constellations' and 'signs'. The former refers to the actual groups of stars as we see them: the latter is a more abstract concept in which the twelve divisions are seen as being equal, each occupying 30° of arc. Moreover, in the latter case, which is the system used in astrology, the vernal point is considered to be constant, always lying at 0° in the sign of Aries. (The vernal or spring point is the point in the zodiac where the sun stands when it is exactly overhead on the equator, when day and night are of equal length over the whole earth). In fact this point changes a little each year in relation to the fixed stars according to 'the precession of the equinoxes'; it takes the sun a 'Platonic year' of 25,920 earth years to make the complete circuit. At the present time the vernal point is in the Fishes and is moving slowly towards the Waterman. There is of course a corresponding point in the autumn in the constellation of the Virgin: this is the vernal point for the Southern Hemisphere.

The confusion in terms can be avoided to a certain extent by referring to the signs by their Latin names and to the constellations by the English equivalents. When working with nature on the land it seems preferable to use the constellations, for variability and uniqueness are nature's attributes, and in her realm nothing is ever exactly delimited. (A diagram and a fuller explanation can be found in Maria Thun's *Work on the Land and the Constellations*.)

The Sun

The heavenly body which has the greatest influence on the growth of plants is of course the sun. In the temperate regions of the Northern Hemisphere one can feel it drawing the plants up to a climax as it gets higher and higher in the sky from midwinter to midsummer, passing through the zodiac from the Goat to the Twins. As it starts to descend, passing through the fiery Lion and into the quieter influence of the Virgin, the forces of growth begin to wane and a period of ripening sets in. Quick-growing vegetables such as lettuce and radish change their character and nowadays we plant different varieties of them more adapted to the shortening days. At this time we ourselves can experience an inner harvest as we gather in and store our crops. In autumn the earth herself draws in the life forces received from the sun during the summer, and during the winter months they make her inwardly alive, preparing for the upsurge of the following spring. The tropical sun also has its moods, drawing life-giving rain behind it as it moves from south to north and back again.

All these are but outer aspects of deeper truths, for there is far more in the sun's rays than the light which we experience through our eyes and the warmth which we feel (or do not feel!) on our bodies. The sun is the only true giver of life on earth. In the plant world not only does the sun's radiation call forth the green colour of the leaves and provide the energy for photosynthesis, but it also carries the forces which shape and form the various organs and those which direct its whole metabolism. Rudolf Steiner, contrary to current scientific belief, frequently described the sun as being 'less than empty', as being a huge concentration of what was called levity in the previous chapter. There is not much we can do in a practical way to guide the sun's activity, but the development of a feeling for it can be a great help in our work on the land.

The Moon

From earliest times it has been observed that the moon affects plant growth. Broadly speaking, it was thought that plants bearing their crop above the ground did best when sown during a waxing moon while root crops preferred a waning moon. The Malays believed that rice should be sown over the period of new moon because a full moon sowing produced very lush growth more attractive to field rats and other pests. During the present century a great deal of experimental work has been done on dates of sowing and planting and also on the timing of cultivations. Significant results have been obtained under carefully controlled conditions on small plots, but sometimes the conclusions of different workers seem to be conflicting. One fact does appear to be fairly certain: the effects are partially or wholly negated by the use of artificial fertilisers and agricultural poisons which deaden the soil's sensitivity and responsiveness. It seems possible that there may be local variations in the extent to which a soil with its underlying rock is able to react to stimuli coming from the moon, and one cannot entirely rule out the possibility of subconscious human influences coming into play.

In this field the work of Maria Thun is outstanding. She began by noting the effects on subsequent growth when seeds were sown with the moon standing in front of the different zodiacal constellations, and found that the earth constellations, Bull, Virgin and Goat, stimulated root development; the water constellations, Fishes, Crab and Scorpion, leaf development; the air constellations, Twins, Scales and Waterman, flowering; and the warmth constellations, Ram, Lion and Archer, seed and fruit. Subsequently it appeared that these effects are modified by other moon rhythms such as ascending and descending, apogee and perigee, and the nodal cycle. Finally she found that certain planetary aspects have to be taken into consideration. Her later work has covered the timing of all cultural operations including transplanting, pruning, harvesting and so on, together with the application of the bio-dynamic sprays. The position has therefore become rather complicated and the bio-dynamic gardener has three choices before him. Aided by her calendar he may attempt to follow all the various rhythms and aspects in full consciousness, or he may decide to follow the calendar blindly, or else he may reach a compromise of his own bearing his local weather and soil characteristics in mind.[1]

Another worker in this field was Franz Rulni and he was the first to produce a calendar which included advice on the mating of livestock in addition to all farming and gardening operations. He emphasised the contrasting effects of the ascending and

1 See M. Thun, *Working with the Stars. Annual Bio-Dynamic Sowing and Planting Calendar.*

descending rhythm, that is to say the roughly fortnightly periods in each month when the moon, irrespective of phase, more or less follows the sun's path as it moves up from the Goat to the Twins and down from the Crab to the Archer. The former is the better time for sowing seeds, the latter for transplanting and cultivations. This rhythm was only more recently incorporated in the Thun calendar. Rulni considered that the adverse effects of eclipses on sowing may sometimes last for a week or more, but Thun only avoids the day of an eclipse. Rulni set great store on the usually favourable influences of the monthly Moon/Saturn oppositions, but occasionally there are adverse factors operative at such times.[1]

Finally L. Kolisko who was one of the first to investigate moon effects, recommended sowing two days before full moon. With such a plethora of experience and advice before him it seems that perhaps the essential thing for the gardener is to try to develop a feeling for the moon's movement, especially by direct observation, and to time his work as far as possible in conjunction with the major rhythms, which I have described in greater detail elsewhere.[2]

The important work of Agnes Fyfe covers a field which is possibly of less significance for the practical aspects of gardening, but which nevertheless helps towards a more comprehensive understanding of lunar and planetary influences. She began with the intention of trying to discover the times when the lunar forces are at their strongest in the sap of mistletoe (used as part of the Iscador treatment for cancer); hellebore and iris are included in many of the tests as comparisons. Using the method of capillary dynamolysis, or chromatography as it is generally called, on samples taken at 8 a.m. every morning over many years, she finds that the formative power is generally stronger when the moon is following a low path, that is when its course through the zodiac is below that taken by the sun. Strangely enough, the power of the FULL moon is weaker at perigee (nearest to the earth) than at apogee (farthest away); the power of the NEW moon in these positions is the opposite—strong at

1 This calender has not been available since Franz Rulni's death.
2 J. Soper: *Studying the Agriculture Course.*

perigee and weak at apogee. Varying but quite definite effects are revealed during eclipses of both sun and moon. Generally speaking there is a marked weakening in the force forms for a few hours over the period of an eclipse even though it may only be visible on the other side of the earth. The complicated moon rhythms are very clearly explained by J. Schultz in *Movement and Rhythm of the Stars* and by N. Davidson in *Astronomy and the Imagination*.

The Planets

To the well-trained intuitive eye the influences of the planets can be seen both in the development of plants and in their forms of growth. Though affected to a certain extent by all the planets, most plants, but especially trees, come strongly under the auspices of one or other of them. Herbalists throughout the ages have known this and have used such knowledge to judge the best times for gathering the ingredients of their medicaments: the classic work of Culpeper on this subject is well known. Another connection brought down from olden times is the relationship of the true metals to the seven planets of the solar system for example, lead—Saturn, tin—Jupiter, iron—Mars, gold—Sun, copper—Venus, mercury—Mercury and silver—Moon. (From a geocentric point of view the moon is a planet.) Making use of this relationship, Agnes Fyfe has shown how the formative forces in the sap of mistletoe, hellebore and iris are not only influenced by the various moon rhythms (including the eclipses), but also by the movements of Mercury and Venus. Following a different line, L. Kolisko demonstrated the beneficial effects of tin salts at high potencies on the germination and growth of sunflowers which, contrary to their name, are Jupiter plants; the other planetary metals had adverse effects.

From Rudolf Steiner's *Agriculture* we learn of the contrasted working of the inner and outer planets: Moon, Mercury and Venus strongly influence the processes of reproduction and growth, while the outer planets, Saturn, Jupiter, and Mars, are more concerned with qualities such as nutritive value, taste, colour, aroma and so on. Planetary rhythms are discernible in the number of petals in the flower. Compare some members of the lily family—for example, the tulip, or the snowdrop with its perianth of three petals and three sepals (the sepals resembling petals)—with the diagram of the loops of Mercury. Then take flowers with five petals, especially the rose family with brambles, crab-apple, cinquefoils and so on, and many of the

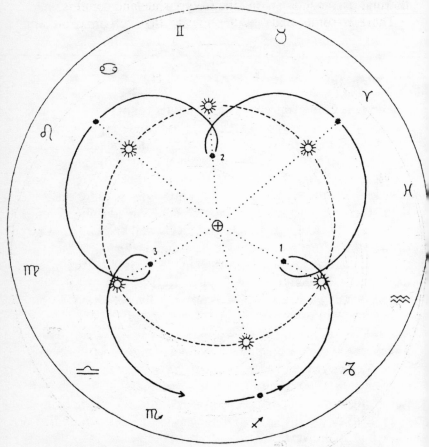

Movement of Mercury in relation to the Earth and Sun during a little less than one year.
Mercury passes through three inferior conjunctions with the Sun as it makes its three inner loops bringing it nearer to the Earth. The path of the Sun is indicated by _ _ _ and the conjunctions by . . . . It also makes three large outer loops, thus passing through three superior conjunctions.

The whole pattern suggests the floral pattern of the three- and six-petalled flowers such as those of the lily family, narcissus, iris, etc. The perianth of six petals is really three petals and three sepals combined, clearly visible in the snowdrop.

buttercup family. Compare them with the diagram of Venus's five loops, and look at the core of an apple cut across transversely. These rhythms are also to be seen in the way the leaves arrange themselves around plant stems (phyllotaxis), and also in the spirals traced by the bracts and reproductive organs of many flowers, particularly among the Compositae and conifers.

There is some evidence to indicate that certain planetary

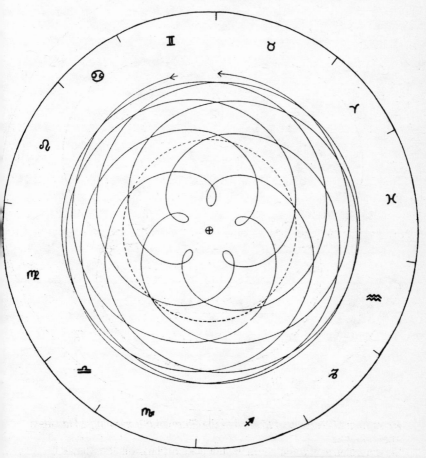

The cyclic rhythms of Venus in relation to the Earth during eight years. The path of the Sun is indicated by _ _ _. The five inner loops of Venus suggest a relationship to the many five-petalled flowers. The same influence is also visible in the phylotaxis of leaves, i.e. the spiral arrangement of leaves up the stalk where the sixth leaf appears directly above the first. This can be seen particularly clearly in the rose where the five-fold succession even continues into the sepals.

aspects and combinations are propitous or the reverse. There is, however, not much the average gardener can do in a positive practical way to make use of these influences other than to follow calendars prepared by experts; in time he may come to experience the weaving of the heavenly bodies himself and to work according to his own intuitions.

CHAPTER 3

Soil

It is a mistake to try to think of the soil as an entirely separate entity which can be divorced from plants. The creation of soil is a mutual interplay between the plant kingdom, the climate and the rocky part of the mineral kingdom. The lowest types of plant life start the soil-forming process when lichens and then mosses become established on a rock face. Their decaying residues produce weak acids which dissolve parts of the rock, and gradually conditions become favourable for slightly higher plants to grow; their roots also secrete acids as they penetrate into cracks in the rock, thus accelerating the process. Although nearly all soils are created in this way originally, rainwater and streams may carry some away and deposit it elsewhere to form alluvial soils. Some soils have also been transported from their place of origin by glaciers, and everywhere there is a small but steady fall-out of dust brought by wind and rain. The surprising extent of such fall-out is well demonstrated when one examines moss which has grown on an asbestos roof, or when one studies the scum on the last remnants of a snow drift.

The soil/plant relationship can be seen from yet another angle. If we compare plants with animals, one of the many differences is that plants have no digestive system. Animals consume food and digest it in a variety of ways, eventually taking the products of digestion into their bodies through the walls of the intestine and other organs. The interior of the digestive tract is not actually a part of their bodies, but is an enclosed space which can open to the world outside. So far as plant/soil is concerned the 'food' consists of the remains of plant and animal life which are taken into the soil and digested by its population of micro-organisms; the products of this digestion pass into the soil water and are absorbed by the root hairs of the plants which thus operate like an intestinal wall. So our main concern when working in the garden is to create and maintain a healthy living soil. If we can achieve this, the plants will to a large extent look after themselves, provided of course that we pay proper attention to their connections with the seasons and to their spatial requirements.

Physical Constituents

From a practical point of view it is an advantage to know something about the origin and nature of the soil with which one is working. The way in which a soil will react to human treatment and to the vagaries of the weather will depend largely on the size of the particles which compose it. Apart from stones and pebbles, these can vary from coarse sand down to fine clay. To give some idea of the very wide range of sizes, the average numbers of the different types of particle required to make an inch (2.5 cm) when placed end to end are given in the table below:

Coarse sand	(2–0.2 mm diameter)	250
Fine sand	(0.2–0.02 mm diameter)	2,500
Silt	(0.02–0.002 mm diameter)	25,500
Clay	(less than 0.002 mm diameter)	50,000 upwards

It is possible to have a mechanical analysis done which will show the percentages of each constituent, but this does not get one much further forward, and a couple of rough simple tests will yield all the information usually needed in practice. For the first of these tests, take a sample of moist but not wet soil about the size of a golf ball, knead it in the palm of your hand and then squeeze it all together into a lump. While doing this notice how gritty it feels, thus getting a fair idea of the amount of coarse and fine sand there is. If the lump fails to cohere, then you know that sand particles predominate; if it can be moulded, clay and silt are the major constituents; if it is on the border of coherence, there is a good balance between coarse and fine.

In the second test, take a tall, rather narrow glass jar of the kind often used for pickles, and put into it a powdered sample a little larger than the previous test, almost fill it with water and shake it thoroughly until it is free of lumps. Then put it on a windowsill and watch how the soil settles out. The coarse sand will sink to the bottom at once, followed very shortly by the fine sand; silt will take rather longer and it may even take a day or two for the finest clay to settle and for the water to become almost clear. A study of the different layers at the bottom of the jar will give you quite a good idea of the proportions which make up your soil.

What is the object of these tests? If you have a soil with a high proportion of sand, you will know that it will almost certainly drain easily and will not create problems of waterlogging. It will not hold a great deal of water in reserve for your plants, but on the other hand what there is will be easily available. It will be a light soil to cultivate and you will be able to work it quite soon after heavy rain without doing any damage. Also it will warm up quickly in the spring. On the debit side, compost and manure will disappear rather rapidly. As far as possible such soils should be kept covered with growing plants, a cover crop or weeds if there are no vegetables or flowers on it; this will ensure that nutrients will be kept in circulation and will not be leached out by rain into the drainage water.

A heavy clay soil will probably have drainage problems, so it is essential to create and maintain an open structure so far as the conditions permit; in extreme cases it may be necessary to put in tile drains to get the surplus water away. Clay soils retain much more water than sands, but it is held more tightly and the plant roots are unable to make use of it all during a drought. Cultivations can be difficult and have to be very carefully timed. If they are done when the soil is too wet it will become 'puddled' and impervious to air and water movement; once this has happened it may take some time to repair the damage. If conditions are too dry, it will be impossible to break up the clods and get a good tilth for sowing or transplanting. Often there are only one or two days when things are just right; these opportunities must be thankfully seized—they may not recur for a month or more. If hard clods have formed in the spring or summer, a heavy shower will loosen them and so will a thorough spraying from a hose. A clay soil will hold nutrients more firmly than a sandy one and it is not so important to keep it covered during the winter; in fact it is often advisable to turn it over in the autumn, forming it into ridges so that a maximum surface of clods is exposed to the disintegrating influence of frost and snow.

On a heavy soil in particular it is often quite a good plan to divide up the vegetable garden into raised beds about 120–150 cm (4–5 ft), wide and about 15 cm (6 in) high, leaving 30–45 cm (12–18 in) paths between. In this way it is seldom necessary to tread on the productive soil and the danger of compaction is avoided. Such an arrangement helps the drainage, and there are very few crops which cannot be fitted in. On sloping land the beds should be constructed along the contours.

There are several different kinds of clay. The worst of these from the grower's point of view is kaolin—the kind used for pottery although it is not always grey or white in colour. Kaolin sets very hard when it dries out, it is not naturally quite so fertile as the others and is the least responsive to remedial measures. Montmorillonite shrinks more on drying and so leaves vertical cracks in the soil: but it is inherently fertile, as is the sort of clay combined with flints which is often formed overlying solid chalk.

Between the two extremes of sand and clay comes a very wide range of soils classified as loams. Around the mid-point of this range are the ideal types of soil for gardening; they have most of the advantages of the extremes and few of the snags. It is however advisable to keep them covered as with the sands and to avoid all unnecessary trampling or compaction as for clay.

Chemical Properties

Some people, particularly those who follow conventional ideas, regard a chemical analysis of their soil as an essential aid towards proper treatment; but for most gardeners it is quite unnecessary to indulge in this rather expensive exercise. For one thing, Dr E. Pfeiffer showed that soil samples from the same field varied very appreciably according to the time of the year when they were taken, and this seasonal variability was fully confirmed by tests done on the Soil Association's farms at Haughley in the Sixties. On organically treated soils with no artificial fertilisers being used it is quite remarkable how the main nutrients rise to a peak at just the times when the crops need them. In some districts it may happen that one of the main nutrients is in short supply: if this is the case there is no doubt that experienced local growers will know about it, and if necessary steps can be taken to rectify matters. Deficiencies of this sort can also come to light through typical discolourations in the foliage of many plants, both annuals and perennials. Professional advice should be sought if unusual colours or disfigurations begin to appear regularly on more than one species of plant. Minor or trace element deficiencies are unlikely to appear on established bio-dynamic gardens; in the early stages they can usually be rectified by foliar sprays. Major element troubles are best cured by the use of rock dusts either through the compost or even by direct application. The use of soluble compounds is not recommended because they bypass natural processes which may atrophy as a result.

There is, however, one important aspect of soil chemistry which is shown up by analysis: this is the acid, neutral or alkaline reaction of the soil water, extremes of which can be very detrimental to optimum growth. A perfectly sound working guide to this feature can be obtained with a quite simple do-it-yourself kit, and good indications can also be derived from a study of the prevalent kinds of weeds. It is usually measured by a logarithmic function of the number of free hydrogen ions in the soil water and is expressed by the symbol pH. A value of 7.0 is neutral and ideal for most crops. 8.0 is getting rather alkaline and is far too high for some plants though welcomed by a few others. 5.5 is definitely acid and is very near the limit which worms will tolerate, while values of 5.0 or lower call for early remedial measures except where heathers, rhododendrons and some other ornamentals are being grown. Immediate amelioration can be achieved by a dressing of quick lime or slaked lime at up to as much as 1 lb per sq yd or 500 g per sq. m. in very acid conditions. This would be a rather violent and drastic way of dealing with the situation, and could have serious repercussions by locking up other nutrients. A more gentle treatment would be an application of not more than 500 g per sq m (1 lb per sq yd) of limestone dust, preferably dolomitic, and this could be supplemented by the inclusion of a greater amount than usual of similar material in the compost heaps.

Generally speaking, sandy soils are more likely to develop acidity than loams or clays, but if a clay type of soil does become very acid it gets stickier than ever and quite intractable for easy working: this is also a feature of clays having a higher than usual sodium content. On the whole the bio-dynamic gardener need not worry unduly about acidity for it has been shown that regular use of the horn manure preparation (see Chapter 6) can steadily raise the pH especially in the region of 5.5–6.5. A flourishing population of earth worms can also be an improving factor. Their casts often contain a high proportion of calcium, the source of which is currently being investigated by research workers.

Aeration, Drainage and Soil Structure

No matter how ideal its mechanical composition or how correct its acidity, a soil will not be able to consummate its union with the plant world unless it can breathe freely and regulate its water relations satisfactorily. It must have the right kind of structure which will allow the free passage of air to the plant roots and soil organisms, and also the free passage of surplus water into its lower layers while at the same time providing enough for the needs of its plant cover. To create and maintain such a structure is therefore one of the most important aims of the bio-dynamic, or for that matter of any, gardener. This aim is achieved firstly by ensuring that there is a sufficient amount of the best kind of humus in the soil, secondly by encouraging the worm population and finally by avoiding any action which might damage the structure by compaction.

Well made bio-dynamic compost contains a comparatively stable type of humus which has the property of being able to bind the soil particles into 'crumbs' of all kinds of shapes and sizes. A certain amount of clay is also necessary for crumb formation, and on very sandy soils it may be advisable to add some clay, perhaps as a slurry to the compost, if a source of good clay is readily available. It is also possible to purchase (at a price) all kinds of clay in powder form from specialist firms. It is not difficult to visualise how larger particles such as crumbs will pack more loosely in the soil than smaller particles, and so leave larger gaps to form the maze through which water and air can circulate.

Soil Water

One cannot help experiencing a deep feeling of wonder and reverence when looking at the way in which Nature has solved the apparently contradictory problems of supplying the soil and plant roots with both the air and the water that they need. Plants use water in three ways. First for circulating the products of soil digestion to where they are needed and also the products of photosynthesis from the leaves to the actively growing parts of stems, roots and so on. Second, for maintaining turgor in the leaves and keeping them cool by evaporation. And third, it is an essential ingredient in the synthesis of sugars and starch by the action of light and chlorophyll. To give some idea of the quantities involved it is estimated that an average crop of wheat needs roughly 450 tonnes of water per acre or half-hectare from sowing to harvest; 99 per cent of this has to come through the soil, only a little being directly absorbed by the leaves from rain or dew.

When it rains the water can either be taken up by the soil or it will run off over the top. In the latter case it will take precious soil with it, so the gardener must do everything possible to prevent this happening. Hard compacted soil will clearly not be able to absorb much water, and run-off may start from patches of this sort; so always loosen soil which may have been trodden down when sowing or planting out. Soil can also become 'capped' by the beating action of heavy rain (also by irrigation sprinklers); the soil crumbs on or near the surface are broken up and the spaces between them get blocked by the finer particles. In severe instances run-off will occur, but in any case soil aeration will be impeded. Again, the answer is to keep the soil covered as far as possible. The most dangerous time for capping is just after sowing and before the germinating crop has started to grow vigorously; keep a sharp look out and use the hoe whenever necessary to break the cap. A very common situation for capping to occur is a clean-weeded onion or leek bed as the leaves are too narrow to provide a good shield; the best solution is to grow them in a mulch.

When rainwater enters a soil, it tends to sink down until it reaches the water table or an underground water channel but only after what is known as the 'water-holding capacity' has been fully topped up. As mentioned earlier, clay soils have a greater capacity than sands and the capacity of all soils is improved by a high organic matter content. Water is held in the upper regions of the soil partly in very fine channels called capillaries (Lat. *capilla* = a hair), partly by being absorbed by the soil colloids—humus and clay. (Colloids are substances, as a rule very complex, which cannot form true crystals in their dry state—glue and gelatine are examples. They are able to absorb water into which they expand and become suspended as opposed to being dissolved.) The water table begins where all the spaces between the soil particles are filled with water: it may be a long way down, but it can be quite close to the surface. In the latter case urgent steps are necessary to lower it because roots cannot grow and will eventually die in a saturated soil: earthworms are killed, and all other soil life comes to a halt. Such a condition becomes obvious if water begins to seep into a shallow hole or trench; if it persists for a week or two after heavy rain, this is an indication that some form of artificial drainage is advisable. As water in the top layer of soil becomes depleted by evaporation and root absorption, more rises up through the capillaries from below in the same way that a piece of string gets moist when suspended over water with an end below the surface.

In dry weather there is always a temptation to resort to the hose or the sprinkler before it is really necessary. Some plants, particularly the brassicas, tend to wilt a little around mid-day in hot weather even though there is still adequate water in the soil. Before deciding to irrigate it is a good plan to dig down a few inches and see by the feel of things whether there is a definite shortage; a little experience will enable one to judge this. If the decision to irrigate is taken, then it is best to do the job thoroughly and give the ground a really good soaking. Half measures are often worse than none at all because the plants will make a lot of surface roots which will continually demand more and more water. Translated into greenhouse practice this means that a thorough watering of the beds once or twice a week is much better than a daily douche. For widely spaced plants such as tomatoes it is a sound plan to sink 10 cm (4 in) pots between each pair of plants and to apply most of the water through these.

Soil Life

Besides partaking in the general life of the earth itself and thereby influencing the behaviour of warmth and air which come in from outside, the soil also sustains a vast army of living creatures ranging from large worms down to bacteria which are only visible under a powerful microscope. The total weight of the living fauna and flora in a fertile pasture is on a par with that of the maximum number of stock which it can carry. Ideally this host of worms, centipedes, mites, springtails, eelworms, amoebae, protozoa, fungi, bacteria and many others form a dynamically balanced whole, each species having its own part to play. Between them they are responsible for the whole of the digestive process mentioned earlier, converting plant and animal corpses (including their own) either into soluble substances which can be taken up through the plant roots or into colloidal humus. Under perfect conditions all these species would be considered beneficial and one could look upon them as providing that combination of influences and qualities, varying with soil and climate, which Nature always strives to attain. Their numbers are usually flexible so they can increase or decrease quite rapidly to meet minor abnormalities caused by man or the environment. But sometimes the strains may be too great and the ideal balance is seriously disturbed. Soluble artificial fertilisers, for instance, make some species redundant and they atrophy, leaving gaps in the pattern which may all too easily be filled by undesirable substitutes. The remnants of any fungicides falling off treated plants will cause similar gaps. In a more subtle way, if there are insufficient numbers of worms, for instance, the necessary 'worminess' may be supplied by other creatures of the same kind, such as destructive larvae. There are both beneficial and harmful eelworms. Or again, if there is not enough decaying organic matter to maintain the right proportion of saprophytic fungi, parasite types may come in and will attack plant roots.

A very special group of fungi known as mycorrhyza is now coming more and more into the limelight. These fungi act as intermediaries between the soil and the plant. Their hyphae (fine hairs) penetrate both the soil and the plant cells in the surface layers of the roots. They can secrete substances from the plant into the soil, and can transfer to the plant complex substances both beneficial and otherwise which would not normally be taken up from the soil solution through the root hairs. At one time it was thought that these fungi were confined to the conifers; then they were found on the roots of deciduous trees, and now they are turning up on quite a lot of annuals as well. They are encouraged by applications of well made compost and are discouraged by artificial fertilisers. Be it noted here that the soil is the true home of fungi, a fact which will influence our attitude to plant diseases discussed in a later chapter.

There are of course many insect species, especially beetles, whose larvae must develop in the soil and may do damage to plants in the process. Two examples are wireworms, larvae of the click beetle, and cutworms which eventually turn into yellow underwing moths. If one considers the fairly common occurrence of these species and the comparatively rare appearance of their larvae in the garden, it seems just possible that they normally breed in pasture or waste land, and only invade a garden when Nature needs them to correct a qualitative imbalance.

Many large books have been written about the various aspects of soil which have been mentioned in this brief and by no means comprehensive account. Suggestions for further study on conventional lines are given in the bibliography at the end. The intention here has been partly to arouse the interest of the novice as opposed to the experienced gardener, and partly to stress certain features where bio-dynamic thinking can give a more satisfying account than the ideas generally accepted at the moment. And here is a final thought: the achievement of a balanced harmony beneath the soil surface will be greatly assisted by aiming at a diversified plant and animal population above.

CHAPTER 4

Water

Water is such a common universal substance that there is a danger of familiarity breeding contempt. In the Western world we demand it as a right and expect to get as much as we want in the cheapest possible way; when we have used and fouled it, we expect it to be removed again in the cheapest possible way. It is treated like any other common dead substance without worrying about its wider functions in the biosphere. And yet water comprises a very large proportion of the weight of every living creature. It is high time that we tried to recover a fuller recognition of its importance, to live more with it, to appreciate its qualities and consciously to work with it. We might think about it occasionally when we use it—where did it come from, where will it go to, why are we using it, are we demanding too much of it?

Chemically speaking water is one of the simplest of substances, and everybody knows its chemical formula H_2O. This means that it is formed by the combination of two volumes of hydrogen with one volume of oxygen; in atomic terms a molecule of water consists of two hydrogen atoms joined to one oxygen atom. This does not tell the ordinary person very much; but we can get some idea of its nature, of its qualities, if we look on this combination as a kind of marriage between the highly expansive power of hydrogen and the contractive, earth-anchoring force of oxygen. Sometimes one, sometimes the other preponderates, thus providing an ideal vehicle for absorbing and transmitting vital rhythms, for carrying the streams of life.

One of the best known physical properties of water is that it is the only naturally occurring earthly substance which expands when it changes from the liquid to the solid state (freezes). This means that ice, being lighter, always forms on the top of a body of water and so there is usually liquid left down below in which life can continue. This property is also important from the gardener's point of view. When a soil with a high proportion of clay becomes frozen, the soil water held between the fine platelets of clay expands and loosens them; the loosening effect remains after the thaw and so improves the soil structure. In a similar way the pressure exerted by freezing water retained in rock crevices is another important disintegrating factor leading to soil formation. From the opposite point of view, do not leave any watery solutions lying around in glass or china containers during the winter in the garden; ice formed during a hard frost will probably shatter the container.

In addition to being a solvent or vehicle for transporting substances, water has another more subtle and perhaps more important function as a carrier of forces and forms. At first sight this may seem rather a far-fetched claim; but anyone who has stood on a bridge watching flowing water should have no reservations about accepting it. The way in which vortices and wave patterns are taken up, played with for a while, and then discarded only to give place to others is surely quite convincing. T. Schwenk, in his book *Sensitive Chaos*, has illustrated in many beautiful ways this form-creating power of water, and has demonstrated how these appearing and disappearing forms correspond with those of human and animal organs, suggesting that water must play a large part in bringing them into being during the embryonic growth period.

It is this form-creating property which seems to be utilised in the preparation of homoeopathic remedies. After making the 24th decimal potency there is theoretically not a single atom or molecule of the original substance left, yet in some way as yet not fully understood, much higher dilutions can have marked effects on living systems. The current explanation is that the water molecules arrange themselves in corresponding patterns; an infinite number of patterns is then theoretically possible, and this gets over the difficulty that a huge number of different patterns would be necessary to cover all the possible potencies which can be made. But this does not explain how the patterns can have an effect in practice. The point to bear in mind here is that they are inoperative in the purely mineral world: only when they are applied to living systems can effects be observed. When we come to discuss in the next chapter the forces operative in the plant kingdom, perhaps a clearer picture will emerge. In the meantime be it noted that the bio-dynamic method uses this power of water to spread the effects of certain preparations for treating soil and plants.

The urge of water to dissolve all kinds of substances and carry them around makes it very difficult to purify completely. The distilled water one uses for topping up batteries is by no means chemically pure, and even doubly distilled water still needs further electrical treatment before it can be used for delicate experiments. By this time it is completely 'dead', but even so it has to be carefully sealed up for storage because if left exposed to the air it will in due course develop a green algal slime. The way in which these algae get the various chemical elements necessary for life will become clearer in the next chapter when the growth of Spanish moss is described.

In the garden and greenhouse we naturally want to use water which contains the fewest harmful impurities and which has the strongest possible forces for the development of life. For irrigation we probably have little choice and will have to make do with what comes through the mains. If this is applied as a fine spray through a sprinkling device, it will lose to the air the remains of any chlorine which may have been added as a sterilant; but there is unfortunately no way of eliminating fluoride if this has been added. Otherwise rainwater is usually recommended as being the least contaminated; but this may not always be the case, especially if the rain clouds have passed over large conurbations such as London or the Black Country in the Midlands. Some rather inconclusive experiments conducted at Clent with germinating cress and wheat seeds indicated that sometimes tap water exposed to the air for an hour or two produced better early growth than rainwater. Some people may be lucky enough to have access to a spring rising from an uncultivated hillside, but well water should be tested before use because it can become contaminated with unutilised nitrogenous fertilisers if the surrounding land is being farmed conventionally. At best only 40 per cent of added nitrogen is taken up by an arable crop; about half the remainder goes off in the drainage water and soil micro-organisms return the rest to the air as gaseous nitrogen.

In days gone by gardeners used to make a point of collecting rain which fell during thunderstorms. That this water should have special living properties is not surprising in view of what Ernst Lehrs has to say about thunderstorms in his book *Man or Matter*, in which he postulates that thunder rain has been newly condensed out of the cosmos. It is also possible to obtain specially active water by causing rainwater to flow in an open channel from one container to another for a few minutes just before and after the exact time of the full moon. It has been shown that seed germinates quicker if watered with water that has been exposed to the full moon for a night. Again, some extravagant claims have been made for the vital activity of water which has been 'charged' through an unusual type of electric condenser using beeswax as the dielectric. Conversely, farmers who use irrigation water from large dams claim that it has a deadening effect on crops immediately below the dam and that it needs to flow freely for at least a mile before it regains its life. That this claim may have some substance is borne out by experimental work with 'flow forms' based at Emerson College.

In spring and summer, especially if one has a greenhouse, there are often times when the supply of rainwater runs out, so it is a good plan to try to store as much as is feasible. Wooden barrels are ideal for this purpose, but are very expensive nowadays. Plastic is probably the next best alternative as it does not corrode like metal which in the process can contaminate the water with the products of corrosion. Some people, however, believe that any kind of plastic 'deadens' the water, but so far no evidence, either chemical or radiaesthetic, seems to have been brought forward to substantiate this belief. In any case, the water should be kept as dark as possible consistent with providing a satisfactory inlet to the container; if the top of a tank or barrel is left open to the sun and air, green algae will soon start to grow vigorously and will become a nuisance. Another point to bear in mind is that, during a dry spell, quite a lot of dust and dirt will accumulate on the house roofs and so on, from which the water is collected; if a convenient device can be designed, it is a good idea to divert into a drain the first water which comes down from the long-awaited break in the weather.

Finally, in order to deepen our understanding of water's manifold being, let us dwell for a moment on two other remarkable features. The first is the sensitive way in which it reflects Nature's moods and co-operates with them. As examples we may take a slow-moving stream or river in midsummer, the surface of a lake on a clear still night, or the fury of the sea during a storm. The second is the enormous power which water can amass when it collects or is collected in bulk. Under control behind a dam it can give us electricity, but the surging joy with which it escapes from the turbines is an indication of the frustration which it felt at being pent up against its natural tendency to flow, a frustration which it vents in terrifying fashion if the dam should chance to break. Or again the devastating might of a tsunami or tidal wave as it approaches the shore must be one of the most frightening experiences a man can have on earth.

CHAPTER 5

Plants

In order to appreciate fully the reasons for various bio-dynamic practices we have to build up a rather more vivid concept of plants than is customary in conventional thought. They are usually regarded as mechanisms subject only to the same laws as hold good in a physics or chemistry laboratory or in the working of a machine. People seem to be so dazzled by the brilliance of the research into such things as the genetic code and single cell metabolism and by the ideas put forward to explain them, that certain vital more holistic aspects have been overlooked. Each new discovery, though it may appear to provide an answer to a question, more often than not poses further questions. The frontier of the unknown may be pushed back a little, but it remains as impenetrable as ever. Although the processes of growth, reproduction and decay are all deemed to be controlled by various communication networks which switch genes on and off, one is still left with the old Latin conundrum, *Quis custodiet ipsos custodies*? (Who is there to control the controllers?). Who or what is there to read the genetic code and operate the switchboard?

Let us begin by comparing a rock or a crystal with a plant, and for the sake of simplicity we will take an annual plant—it is not too difficult to apply the same concepts to perennials or even to trees. To make the imagination more realistic we might choose at random a definite mineral, say quartz, and a definite plant, say a broad bean. On the one hand the quartz crystal gives us the strong impression that its shape, its beautiful form, has been imposed on it by influences coming from outside; it is a piece of finished work, and can only be changed by some external physical force. The form of the bean plant on the other hand, though just as beautiful in its own way, has quite a different quality; it is never precisely the same from one moment to another, and this continuous change arises from out of itself. What we see at any given time is like one frame of a long ciné film comprising a rhythmic pattern of development, fruition and decay. Even this pattern does not quite represent the whole broad bean which has connections with all past generations and also with the generations still to come. Instead of a static entity like the crystal, we have in the bean plant a centre or focus of highly organised activities. Together with a few of today's leading biologists, we are almost irresistibly led to postulate the supersensible presence of a body of organising formative forces: Rudolf Steiner called this the etheric body. Just as any separate piece of matter has a centre of gravity derived from the whole gravity field of the earth, so every living creature acquires an etheric body derived from the earth's etheric field; this has been described by H. Poppelbaum as a morphogenetic field and can be seen as the link between material manifestation and the higher spiritual worlds beyond. This whole complex of activity, this 'weaving, vibrant, pulsating essence' as Rudolf Steiner put it, is the sphere in which homoeopathic remedies and substances in very high dilutions, as described in the last chapter, are effective.

The etheric body of an individual plant could perhaps be seen as the switchboard operator which earlier we failed to find. It interprets the general pattern of the particular plant and modifies or adapts it to fit into the individual niches in which single specimens are growing. It heals any wounds which may occur, and reacts in the most favourable way to any changes, physical or supersensible, earthly or cosmic, which may take place in the environment. The patterns themselves, the 'ciné films', have their home in the next spiritual plane above the etheric, usually known as the 'astral'.

Continuing our imagination of the bean plant, let us now look at a plant as it stands with its roots reaching down into the earth, its leaves spread to receive the incoming cosmic stream, its flowers opening up to the heavens and to the insect world. Just as the roots merge almost imperceptibly into the soil, into the element earth and water, so leaves and blossoms with their continual interchange of substances can be thought of as merging with the elements air and fire (warmth). The former feel the pulse of the earth's rhythms, the latter connect with the influences of the starry world, with the circling paths of the planets. Selflessly each individual plant passes through time, performing its own special part as a member of the plant kingdom in the cosmic task of giving. Through photosynthesis plants remove carbon dioxide from the air and give out oxygen in its place for the benefit of the earth as a whole and for man and animal in particular. They give their substance in various forms for the nourishment of man and animal including the insects. Some give themselves as healers, some, as we shall shortly see, are there merely to help other plants growing near them. A few, like some rare human beings, create an atmosphere of wellbeing by their mere presence. But whatever people with electrical gadgets and boiling prawns may say, plants have no direct feelings of pleasure and pain like animals or men; they have no organs for such experiences. This does not imply that such experiments have been 'rigged', but just that they have been misinterpreted. In fact if one takes the concept of an etheric field as valid, it would be surprising if the instruments had not reacted under the circumstances described.

If different plants, say a wheat plant, a cabbage, a carrot and a bean, are grown close together so that the roots of each have access to the same soil conditions, if they are subsequently burnt and their ashes analysed chemically, it is quite remarkable how the proportions of the chemical elements in the various ashes are entirely different. Though the amounts will vary slightly according to the soil, the patterns are just as characteristic for each species as are the leaf and floral forms. A plant can select what it needs from the soil in which it is growing, always provided that its needs are there in the first place. There are, however, exceptions. On the one hand, if the soil solution has been affected by the application of soluble fertilisers, the plants may be forced to take up more of certain elements than they require, and their whole metabolism may then be so disrupted that they become sitting targets for pathogenic organisms. On the other hand, some species of plants have as their special function in Nature's household the collection of some one or other of the chemical elements out of the atmosphere. This phenomenon can be seen as a kind of 'depotentisation'—the opposite of potentising—for it seems (contrary to current dogma) that we are surrounded by matter in what E. Lehrs calls 'its imponderable state', or *in statu nascendi* (in a state of becoming). That this is no idle fancy is demonstrated by the Spanish moss (*Tillandsia usneoides*) which grows on telegraph wires in South America out of all contact with the soil. It is vigorous and can be shown to have a full complement of all the major chemical elements together with a wide range of the trace elements. The quantities involved are so large that they could hardly have been absorbed from the sporadic rain which in any case has only the smallest trace of phosphate in it. The only explanation is that substance has been condensed out of the air. It is interesting to record that the opposite process has recently been proved experimentally: pine and pea seedlings have been shown to disperse into the air soil contaminants such as cadmium and zinc.

Experiments on somewhat similar lines were conducted in the former Soviet Union. They grew maize and a type of bean together in mixed stands. On some plots they persuaded the bean to 'fix' a radioactive isotope of nitrogen, and by means of a Geiger counter they very soon found some of this nitrogen in the maize plants. On other plots they sprayed the maize foliage with radioactive phosphate and before long it had found its way into the beans. So it seems that plants not only draw nutrients out of the soil solution, but that they are also able to contribute to this solution for the benefit of plants of other species. Thus a pool of nutrients is created in the soil by the plants growing on it: if their species are diverse and well mixed, the pool will be rich; but in a monoculture or with incompatible species the pool will be nonexistent. These facts shed an interesting light on companion planting, and may also give us cause to revise our ideas about weeds: perhaps they are not so universally bad as is usually supposed.

From our picture of a plant standing between heaven and

earth it is not surprising that sunlight, either direct or obscured by cloud, has a very strong influence on the way in which a plant develops its inherent qualities. Everybody knows how root crops stored in a dark cellar produce elongated, rather shapeless shoots and tiny leaves quite devoid of colour. This is of course an extreme case, but it does indicate how closely plant nature and light nature are interwoven. Some plant species, particularly those belonging to the lower orders such as ferns and mosses, are attuned to cool, shady conditions; but others requiring full sunlight will languish when shaded by taller companions. These facts will influence the planning of a garden and care needs to be taken that taller vegetables do not unduly restrict shorter neighbours; orientating the rows north and south will help to solve this difficulty.

Even more important for the growth of many annuals and perennials is the seasonal effect of longer and shorter days. Some plants need a long day before they can form flower buds, others must have short days. For instance, beetroot bolts if sown too early. Apart from the length of day there are other more subtle differences in the quality of the sun's light according to the constellation of the zodiac in which it is standing at any given time. It is at present difficult to specify these effects for practical planning, but they should always be borne in mind when trying to assess the reasons for unexpected phenomena. Perhaps it is something of this nature which renders groundsel and some other common weeds very susceptible to rust diseases after the middle of August. All this points to the desirability of sowing annual crops so that they mature in their proper season. We have so many plants at our disposal covering the whole year that it is rather unnecessary to try to grow any of them out of season; it is senseless to complain of lack of success, of pest and disease attacks, if one does attempt to do this.

Trees fall into a category rather different from annual and herbaceous plants. One feature, as Grohmann so clearly points out, is that the side shoots of an annual are arranged in a pattern determined by its phyllotaxis (see Chapter 2); the branches of a tree spring from the trunk in patterns quite unrelated to the succession of its leaves on the twigs. The forms created by the branches are characteristic of each individual species, a fact which can be noted with great interest in winter when the deciduous trees have shed their leaves. The whole development of trees takes place in their own special milieu of formative forces.

From an imaginative point of view it is possible to regard the trunks of trees with their main branches as raised mounds of soil, each leaf-bearing shoot and twig being a separate plantlet growing out of this enhanced kind of earth. This is not the place to go more deeply into the idea, and the reader is referred to Lecture VII of *Agriculture*. If, however, the concept is valid, then it would be logical to treat the bark of a tree, especially a fruit tree, in a way somewhat similar to the way we treat the soil. This is in fact done with advantageous effects by applying a fairly stiff paste to the trunks and major branches, as described later in Chapter 14.

In any general account of plant life as seen from the bio-dynamic standpoint it is perhaps fitting to conclude with a description of Goethe's far-reaching observation, conducted over many years and brought to fruition in his *Metamorphosis of Plants*. He was inspired to this study when he asked himself the questions, How do we know that an object in front of our gaze is a plant? What are its essential characteristics? He felt that there must be some universal underlying pattern behind the form and development of every plant species. Contrary to the common practice of starting with the lowest type of plants from which the higher orders are supposed to have evolved, he took his stand at the outset on the higher flowering plants, and saw the lower orders as less successful strivings towards the higher goal. He eventually found the secret in the green leaf with a node at its base. He saw how in many plants the leaves develop from the shapeless cotyledons of the seed, gradually exhibiting their particular form and then withdrawing it as flowering approaches: buttercups and delphiniums are especially good for studying this phenomenon. In other plants the leaf shape is more or less constant from the start. After this display, or sometimes concurrent with it, the leaf forms contract and gather together to make the calyx for the flower. There is an expansion as the blooms open out followed by a contraction into the floral organs, anthers and ovaries; but the latter are in fact

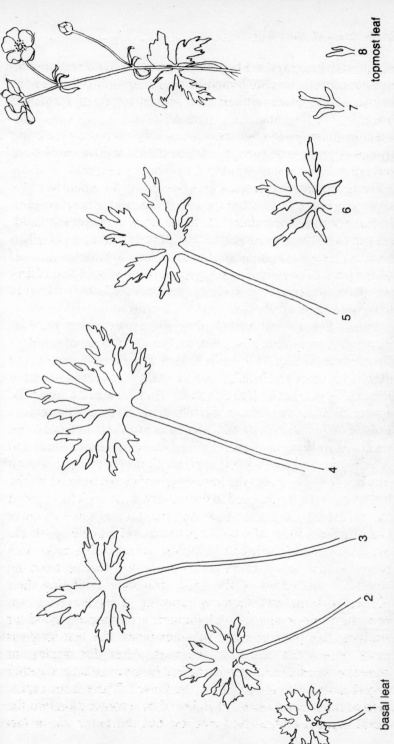

The field buttercup (*Ranunculus acris*), showing the sequence of the leaves. *Drawing: Tabitha Parsons*

basal leaf

1
2
3
4
5
6
7
8 topmost leaf

metamorphosed leaves. One example which led Goethe to this latter conclusion was the comparatively common sight of a small leaf appearing instead of an anther in the flower of a wild rose. After fertilisation another expansion occurs as the fruit and seeds begin to swell; but the carpels enclosing the seeds are again metamorphosed leaves, a fact which is often obvious when picking peas—the leaves look like pods.

Thus Goethe's archetypal plant arose in his mind's eye— expansion into leaf, contraction into flower bud, expansion into flower, contraction into floral organs, expansion into seed and fruit and a final contraction into the ripened seed. This UR plant is not to be seen as a physical primaeval ancestor from which the whole plant kingdom has descended, but is a fundamental pattern in the world beyond the senses, and into it there can flow an infinite number of forms and rhythms to produce different species in the physical world. In the lower plant orders parts of the pattern are omitted or coalesce. Rudolf Steiner developed this theme further to include the root, and glimpses of his adaptations are to be found throughout *Agriculture*. This theme has been extensively elaborated by G. Grohmann who has shown in what ways the lower plant orders—gymnosperms, ferns, mosses and so on—can be seen as less successful strivings towards a more perfect goal.

CHAPTER 6

The Bio-Dynamic Preparations

The Bio-dynamic Preparations fall into two categories: two are
of a general nature and six are for treating compost and manure
(the ninth will be discussed in Chapter 11 dealing with fungus
diseases). They have been given identification numbers which
have no special significance. Their main purpose is to stimulate
and enhance the supersensible forces and influences working in
from the far spaces of the cosmos and up from the centre of the
earth. The methods of making them are fully described by
Rudolf Steiner, but anybody wishing to make them for himself is
strongly advised first to work with an experienced person as
there are many small details which are essential for achieving
the best results. In later references the numbers alone will be
used. (Gardeners are advised to purchase the small quantities
required from the address at the end of this book, or from a local
group. Only farmers find it worthwhile to make their own.)

Preparation 500

This preparation, also known as 'horn manure', is made from
fresh cow dung from grazing, bio-dynamically or organically
managed cattle. It is pressed into cow horns and buried in good,
fertile soil for the whole of the winter period from Michaelmas
to Easter, to absorb cosmic radiation.

The horns of cows are not weapons of defence. Both horns
and hooves are places where certain vital forces connected with
digestion (so important in the cow) are reflected back into the

digestive system. The manure and cosmic forces are therefore contained within the cow horn. What comes out is a dark, odourless, crumbly material which, like all the bio-dynamic preparations, should be kept in peat in a box until used.

The purpose of 500 is to promote root activity, to stimulate the soil micro-life, to regulate the lime and nitrogen content of the soil and to help in the provision of trace elements. Even if this is difficult to understand, try it and see how it works, transforming the soil and invigorating the plants. (If your soil has been deadened by chemical fertilisers or pesticides, persevere and add as much compost or composted manure as you can.)

For one acre a minimum of 4.0 g (1 unit if purchased) is stirred for an hour in about 13.5 litres (3 gals) of lukewarm water. For smaller areas less of the preparation is necessary, but it is not easy to stir less than 4.5 litres (1 gal) effectively. The container used for stirring must be clean and free from all forms of contamination. It can be an earthenware crock, a wooden bucket or barrel, a copper, stainless steel or enamelled bucket or tank. Galvanised vessels are not so satisfactory, and if there is no alternative to plastic choose one of the hard, dense types. The size will depend upon the amount to be stirred, but it should be big enough to avoid splashing during vigorous stirring.

Spring water or clean rainwater is best, but if chlorinated mains water is the only source available it should be exposed to the air for some time and stirred occasionally to get rid of the chlorine. Raise the temperature of the water to bloodheat and rub the preparation between the thumb and fingers in the water so that it is broken down as finely as possible. Stir with a stick chosen to suit personal convenience; a thick stick will create a crater more rapidly than a thin one, but this is not necessarily a good thing. The method of stirring is very important. Stir briskly until a deep crater is formed in the rotating liquid; then quickly reverse the direction of stirring and continue until the deep crater is formed once more. Continue this alternation for one hour, always reversing quickly so that the whirling liquid folds in upon itself in a seething chaotic turbulence.

When stirring has been done for the full hour the liquid should be applied to the soil as soon as possible and not be kept for more than an hour or two. There are several ways of applying it.

For a large garden some form of sprayer is advisable, and in this case the liquid must be strained through gauze or cheesecloth into the container. Straining is not so essential if a syringe with a coarse nozzle is used. Another method is to flick the liquid out of a bucket with a bunch of twigs (conifers are good) or a white-wash brush. There is no disadvantage if the droplets are quite large, but experience is necessary to cover the desired area evenly.

In the garden the spray is applied to all open ground, frames and greenhouse beds in spring and autumn, preferably just before cultivating or spreading compost. It can also be used effectively when preparing seed beds or areas for transplanting. It should always be sprayed on moist soil, never on a dry or frozen surface. The best time of day is late afternoon or evening when the earth is breathing in. During a drought it may be sprayed on the soil between growing plants after sunset in order to increase their root systems.

Preparation 501

This preparation, also known as 'horn silica', is made from very finely ground quartz or feldspar; it is used as a foliar spray to enhance the light and warmth forces, but *only* if 500 has already been applied to the soil. The horn again contains and concentrates radiations. Silica has affinity with light and the sun, and as the horn is buried during the summer it is subjected to an enlivening warmth process. It encourages the plant's development towards the flowering process, whereas 500 encourages root development and growth upwards from the ground. Preparation 501 is particularly helpful at times when sunlight is inadequate. It is stirred in the same way as 500, but for a half-hectare (one acre) only 1g (say enough to cover the tip of a penknife) is sufficient. It is applied as the finest possible mist quite early in the morning as soon as any dew has evaporated, preferably in sunshine. Experience is needed to time the spraying at the best stages of crop growth: a very early application may have an adverse effect. As a general rule spray when that part of the plant which is to be harvested is beginning to develop—for example, lettuce when the heart can just be discerned, peas when flower buds can be seen, potatoes when tubers begin to form, root crops when swelling starts. Root crops at a later stage of development may also be treated in the afternoon or evening. Both soft and top fruit are sprayed at the flower bud stage and again when the fruit is ripening. Few gardeners, however, can afford the time to stir for an hour merely to treat three gooseberry bushes or a short row of peas, so a compromise must be made by choosing a time when several crops are more or less at the best stage. It is to be hoped that before long quicker ways of activating this preparation will be found. The use of 501 not only increases the yield of garden crops, it is also an important agent in enhancing their quality as expressed by aroma, taste, sweetness and keeping potential.

Preparations 502–507

These are commonly known as the compost preparations and are usually supplied as a set. They are made respectively from yarrow flowers, chamomile flowers, stinging nettles, oak bark, dandelion flowers and valerian flowers, treated in various ways. It is not a practical proposition for gardeners to make them themselves as they require to be prepared in certain animal organs, mostly connected with digestive and metabolic processes. These are extremely difficult to obtain owing to slaughterhouse regulations, and the resultant quantities are far more than several gardeners would require. One set is sufficient to treat up to 15 tonnes of compost material or manure (Note: 1 tonne measures from 0.75–1.15 cu. m (1–1½ cu. yds) according to the type of material). The main function of these substances is to radiate forces rather than to supply material. Nevertheless, it is advisable to use a full set even in heaps of less than half the maximum size. For very small heaps it is possible to use only half portions of each preparation; the remaining half portions can be returned to their containers and put away in a cool dark place until the next heap is ready. These preparations should be looked on more as regulators than as activators, as foci through which various forces and influences can work in to create a harmonious whole. Some workers see in each preparation the influence of a different planet.

When treating a completed heap the preparations are not mixed together and placed in one hole, but the individual preparations are put into separate holes evenly spaced around the heap. The holes are made 30–45 cm (12–18 in) deep pointing towards the central core of the heap; a crowbar or thin stake is a good implement for the job, waggling it about to make a reasonably clear hole. Each preparation is then placed at the bottom of its hole either using a spoon tied to the end of a stick or by rolling it into a ball. Cover it with a little mature compost or fine soil and push the material of the heap firmly inwards. Always make sure that the preparation is in intimate contact with its surroundings and not just sitting in an air space. The liquid valerian preparation 507 is added to about a gallon of lukewarm water as for 500, and is stirred vigorously for ten minutes. About a quarter of it is poured down one hole and the rest sprayed with a watering can over the whole heap before covering it. In large heaps for farms or market gardens, requiring more than one set of preparations, the holes should not be more than 90 cm (3 ft) apart.

When a heap is being built in one operation and is about half its finished height the solid preparations can be put in their appropriate places (again with a little mature compost), and the building is continued: this saves the trouble of making holes. Preparation 507 is then applied as previously described. In the case of heaps which are being built gradually it is worthwhile to divide each solid preparation into two parts and to put these half portions in position when the heap is about one third of its expected height. They must be covered at once by a 5–7 cm (2–3 in) layer of material. The remaining half portions are inserted just before completion.

The valerian preparation 507 can be used separately as a protection against expected frost, especially on flowering top fruit. Spray in late afternoon or evening at the rate of one unit in 9 litres (2 gals) of warm water, giving a thorough coverage; the full quantity needed will naturally depend on the number and size of the trees.

When starting to convert an area to bio-dynamic treatment it is a sound plan to stir the compost preparations in with the first application of 500; the minimum rate is one set per half-hectare (acre). This can also be done with advantage when turning in green manure.

These preparations lie at the very heart of bio-dynamic practice and thinking; they are to the whole concept what compost is to the soil. They need to be handled with loving care, not in the casual way in which conventional adjuncts to gardening are used.

The Preparation Plants (*by B. Saunders-Davies*)

502 YARROW FLOWERS (*Achillea millefolium*)
This plant has a beneficial effect on its surroundings even when it is growing wild on the edge of paths and so on. It contains homoeopathically active potash and has a regulating effect on the soil. It is also a mediator of forces of many valuable trace elements. All these preparations contain sulphur in homoeopathic quantities which facilitates the working of other substances. (The term 'homoeopathic quantities' means quantities of a substance so dilute as not to be detectable by scientific analysis.)

503 CHAMOMILE FLOWERS (*Matricaria recutita*)
There is much confusion over the botanical name of this plant, previously called *Matricaria chamomilla* or *Chamomilla officinalis*. Botanists have recently reclassified many plants and its correct name now is as above. It is an annual, sometimes called German chamomile, is very aromatic, with delicate stems and leaves, and often grows in waste places. Once established, it seeds itself freely. To check that you have the right species, cut open the conical flowerhead which is hollow. It is a medicinal herb, good for the digestion, and the preparation regulates the rotting process in the compost heap. It also directs the calcium processes.

504 STINGING NETTLE (*Urtica dioica*)
Rudolf Steiner is high in praise of this plant. He speaks of it as irreplaceable. It carries the radiating forces of potash, calcium, iron and sulphur, it prevents nitrogen escaping from the heap and, in Rudolf Steiner's words, 'makes the soil intelligent'.

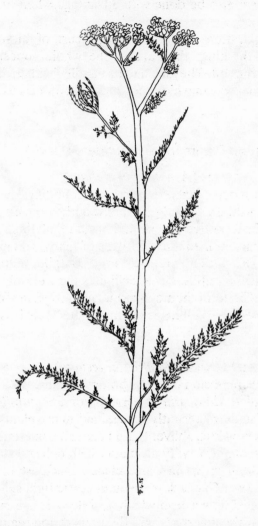

Yarrow (*Achillea millefolium*). Preparation 502. *Drawing: Tabitha Parsons*

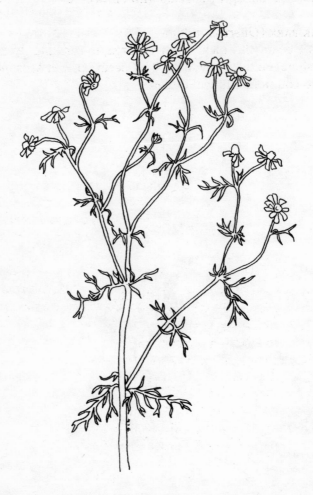

Wild Chamomile (*Matricaria recutita*). Preparation 503. *Drawing*: Tabitha Parsons

A compost of nettles is wonderfully invigorating. The value of nettles as a foliar spray is dealt with elsewhere.

505 OAK BARK (*Quercus robur*)

This is rich in the ideal form of organic calcium. It checks overlush vegetative growth such as occurs in wet seasons and helps to counteract fungal diseases.

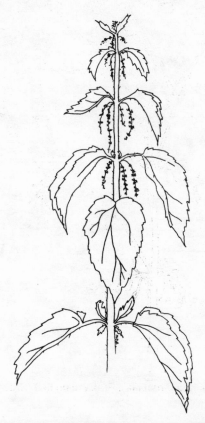

Stinging Nettle (*Urtica dioica*). Preparation 504. *Drawing: Tabitha Parsons*

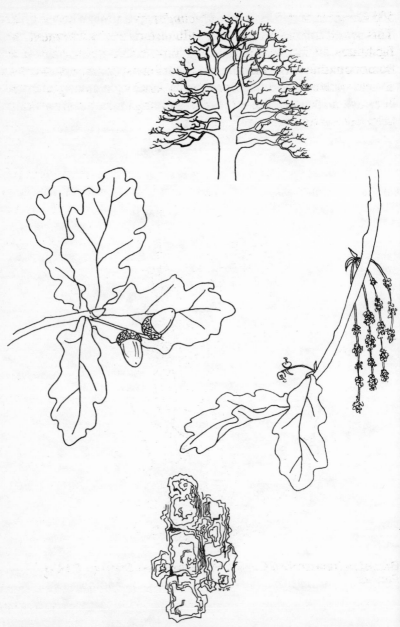

Oak (*Quercus robur*). Preparation 505 is made from the bark only. For identification the drawing above shows, *top* the framework of a mature tree, *centre right* leaves and flower tassles, *centre left* leaves and acorns, and *bottom* the bark. *Drawing: Tabitha Parsons*

506 DANDELION (*Taraxacum officinale*)

This plant also radiates a good influence on its environment. It facilitates an interaction between potash and silicic acid in a homoeopathic way. Silicic acid is distributed homoeopathically in the cosmos. The dandelion is 'a kind of messenger from heaven', as Rudolf Steiner puts it, helping plants to draw what they need from their environment.

Dandelion (*Taraxacum officinale*). Preparation 506. *Drawing: Tabitha Parsons*

507 VALERIAN (*Valeriana officinalis*)

This is the pale pink, wild variety, not the red species of the garden. The sap is pressed from the flower heads. This stimulates the phosphorus process in the manure or compost.

Valerian (*Valeriana officinalis*). Preparation 507. *Drawing: Tabitha Parsons*

CHAPTER 7

Compost

From our discussion on the soil in Chapter 3 it will already have become clear that the key to a successful bio-dynamic garden is a regular supply of high quality humus. Although earthworms can play an important part here, the main source of supply must be well made compost. Some fortunate individuals with 'brown fingers' make very good compost by instinct, but more ordinary mortals have to acquire the art. A great deal of conventional research has been done on the subject and most of the findings are relevant to bio-dynamic work: a suggested reading list is given in Appendix C for those who wish to go deeply into the matter. Only a fairly comprehensive guide to general principles and practice is attempted here, which should hopefully lead most people to the desired goal.

In order to understand these principles in their living context it is first of all necessary to appreciate that a compost heap has— or ought to have—a kind of life of its own, even to the extent that it can be seen as an individual organism. No two compost heaps can ever be exactly alike. Above all a compost heap must have a skin. If a skin of peat, soil, grass or other suitable material is not provided, the heap will of its own accord develop a crusty skin from the dried out materials on its surfaces. The inner life of the heap finds physical expression in a multitude of micro-organisms very similar to those found in a fertile soil but in more concentrated numbers. But circulatory currents and radiations not as yet detected by physical instruments also develop inter-nally, especially those created by the preparations described in the last chapter. So we have to provide the four elements which are essential for all forms of life—food, water, air and warmth—and these must be present in properly balanced proportions.

Food consists of all the materials which we wish to convert into soil nourishment. For those of a scientific turn of mind it may be helpful to know that when organic materials of any kind decompose, they tend towards an end product in which the ratio of carbon to nitrogen is between 15:1 and 12:1. In sawdust, for example, the original ratio is at best 100:1 and often greater; in order to reach 15:1 a great deal of ligneous material will have to be lost, and the final result will show a great reduction in weight. On the other hand poultry manure at about 8:1 will have to lose a lot of precious nitrogen to reach 12:1, hence the smell of ammonia often noticed round heaps of any animal manure. The ideal starting ratio leading to a minimum loss of weight is 30–40:1, and this points to the necessity for a judicious mixture of ingredients.

Water and air are closely related and are dealt with later. The necessary warmth is usually generated in the heap by the initial breakdown processes; it derives from the sun warmth absorbed by plants during their growth. Very small heaps will not heat up, and heating will not be so vigorous in winter as in summer. Sometimes too much heat may develop and the temperature may rise above the optimum 145°F (70°C). This will again be indicated by a smell of ammonia and means that a serious loss of nitrogen is occurring. In this case the heap should be broken down as soon as possible and rebuilt.

The Compost Yard

It is advisable to set aside a definite area of the garden for compost making. The size will naturally vary according to circumstances, but sufficient room should be allowed for three heaps of dimensions adequate to supply the garden's needs—one heap in the early stages, one maturing and one for using—but this arrangement will need seasonal adjustments. Extra space can be included for liquid manure containers and any special composts. The first consideration must be convenience of working; raw materials have to be brought in and the finished compost has to be carted onto the land, so easy and firm access for barrow or trailer is essential. Partial shade is best, and some form of shelter against cold drying winds should be provided, and here a permanent hedge can be useful. But remember that ash trees and privet in particular have an uncanny 'nose' for a compost heap; if either is growing nearby their roots will soon invade and rob a heap. North-south orientation of heaps is good so that both sides are warmed evenly. A well-drained site is vital; water should never be allowed to collect at or around the base of a heap. Finally, all else being equal, a handy water supply can be a great advantage.

Materials and Building

The first detail to settle is the right dimensions of the heap; this will obviously depend upon the size of the garden and the amount of material available. There is a minimum size below which a heap cannot maintain sufficient life and warmth, a relatively large surface allows it to cool and dry out too easily. A base area of about 120 cm (4 ft) square is the lowest possible limit. If there is insufficient material to build a heap of this size within a month, it is better to use a container. For gardens with a

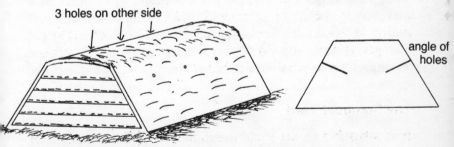

Diagram and vertical section of a compost heap. Layers of compost material about 15 cm (6 in) thick are built up with thin interlayers of soil and a dusting of slaked lime. Three holes are made diagonally into both sides, one for each of the preparations 502–7. They are inserted as described on p. 43. About a quarter of the valerian liquid (507) is poured down one hole with a watering can (with rose removed). The hole can be made vertically to facilitate pouring. The remainder is sprinkled over the whole heap before covering. In very dry climates, if watering is necessary, a shallow depression can be made along the top of the heap.

good supply of material a base of 240 cm (8 ft) with sides sloping to give a width of 45 cm (18 in) at 120 cm (4 ft) high is ideal, the heap being as long as required. On a more modest scale a 180 cm (6 ft) base with sides sloping to a peak at 120 cm (4 ft) will probably be found more convenient. It is far better to start small and enlarge if necessary than the other way round. It is also advisable, especially during the warmer months of the year, to finish off a heap quickly and begin another: otherwise the resulting compost will be unevenly matured.

The best results are obtained if the materials are steadily collected and the heap built in one operation. For materials, anything which will readily decompose is suitable; this includes all refuse and weeds from the garden, lawn mowings, old hay and straw, the coverings from previous heaps, all kinds of kitchen waste, wood (but not coal) ashes, dead leaves (in moderation), and especially any animal or bird manure. Even diseased plants are safe if the heap is well made; beneficial organisms will exterminate pathogens. It is generally not possible to obtain from the house and garden sufficient material to make the desired amount of compost, but various things can be brought in, such as a bag of horse manure from a riding stable, bracken from a hillside or hedge and so on. If municipal compost is bought in, stack it for a month with the preparations before use or put it into a heap while building. Sewage sludge is not recommended except in very small quantities well mixed with other material. On a larger scale the local authority can sometimes be persuaded to dump a load of trimmings from less frequented roads, or there may be opportunities to go out and collect for oneself. Rotting is more even and rapid if the materials are chopped into short lengths of 25–50 mm (1–2 in); this applies especially to long grass. An old chaff cutter is ideal, but a sharp spade or a chopper used on a block made from a section of tree trunk fixed in a vertical position will usually have to do. There are small machines designed for this work, but their robustness is often questionable.

Before starting to build a heap it is essential to prepare the base. Never build a heap on living turf or on hard compacted soil. In the first case skim off the turf and put it into a small heap on its own; it will eventually produce good material for potting mixtures. In the latter case fork over the site leaving the soil loose so that air can get in and water out. As a refinement on well drained soils the base may be dug out to a depth of several inches; the excavated soil is put on one side to provide a covering for the heap when completed, and some can be used in very thin layers when building. A further refinement is to add to the base a little clay on sandy soils or a little coarse sand on clay soils. As emphasised before, make sure that water will not collect in or around the heap.

Start the heap by putting down a layer of well mixed material about 10 cm (4 in) thick. If there is not much nitrogenous stuff present (young weeds, young grass, household scraps, pea or bean haulms) sprinkle a little dried blood or hoof and horn meal over the surface. Alternatively, at this stage a thin layer of poultry deep litter or droppings, or any other available animal excreta should be added. Cover with a thin layer of soil, old compost, peat or a mixture of these, and then sprinkle with slaked lime, or better still with Dolomitic limestone dust. This is also the time to add finely ground basalt or granite, and perhaps rock phosphate if the garden is naturally rather deficient in this element. Then continue adding further layers until the desired size is reached or until the materials are exhausted. Always pack firmly but not too tightly, and never tread on the heap. If the heap is incomplete, cover with straw, old sacking or pieces of carpet until more material is available. The completed heap, after inserting the preparations, should be given a covering of soil, granulated peat or even lawn mowings 2.5–7.5 cm (1–3 in) thick. Finally put on a thick protective covering of straw or bracken which will help to retain the heat and ward off excessive rainfall. It is a good plan now to plunge a stick (such as an old broom handle) or a metal rod more or less horizontally into the heart of the heap with one end projecting; when withdrawn periodically it will give a useful indication of the temperature and also the degree of moisture.

The most important and often the most difficult thing when building a heap is to get the moisture content just right. If it is too dry, very little breakdown is possible. If too wet, a foul-smelling compacted anaerobic mass reminiscent of silage is formed and putrefies into a breeding ground for flies; though eventually worms may work through it, the result will not be of much fertilising value. Ideally the materials should have the consistency of a damp sponge so that, when squeezed in the hand, water just will not seep out. This condition is fairly easy to attain if the materials have been chopped up and thoroughly mixed. If the mixture feels rather dry each layer can be sprayed before adding the extras, but note that deep litter is difficult to moisten. A problem may arise when there is a mixture of green material and old dry stems, and here one has to rely largely on experience. In any case always have water handy and err rather on the moist side than on the dry.

In a small garden where for most of the year the main source of compost material comes from the kitchen, it will seldom be possible to generate any worthwhile heat; in such a case it is probably better to use containers, one for filling, the other for maturing and use. There are several types of bin on the market, but it is not difficult to do it yourself. The chief feature to observe is to allow access for air but at the same time to prevent any warmth from escaping. Solid containers of brick, concrete or wide slabs of wood are therefore not suitable. A good design is to fix four corner posts firmly in the ground and projecting about 120 cm (4 ft) above it; either 5 × 5 cm (2 × 2 in) or 7.5 × 7.5 cm (3 × 3 in) would be suitable. On the outside and inside of

A way of protecting the covering from wind. A post and wire compost bin in the background. *Photo: J. Anderson*

these tie wire netting or some kind of plastic mesh, and fill the interspace with straw or wood wool. Do not fix the netting too firmly as it will be necessary to slip it up the posts for easy access to the finished compost. The soil at the base should be loosened and a bottom layer of coarser material such as hedge clippings will help aeration. Fill the container in much the same way as building a larger heap, but it will take longer, and if there is a lot of kitchen refuse more liberal sprinklings of lime or limestone dust and soil are advisable. Keep a cover of old sacking or carpet on the top and provide some kind of protection from heavy rain up above. Finish off with 5–7.5 cm (2–3 in) of good soil or peat. And here be it noted that peat, in spite of what many advertisments say and although it is of organic origin, contains only very little in the way of plant nutrients.

Long Term Heaps

In many gardens there will be quite appreciable quantities of coarser wastes such as semi-woody hedge clippings, other prunings, old raspberry canes, herbaceous border thinnings, brassica stalks, tufts of couch or other grasses and odd bits of turf. These can be made into long term heaps taking 18–24 months to mature. It is good but not essential to bash up the coarsest items. Such heaps will naturally take quite a long time to complete, but the compost preparations can be put in at about the half-way stage, and it is not vital to provide a covering. Some people may be horrified at the idea of putting couch grass into a compost heap, but the roots are rich in nutrients and it is quite remarkable how they will disappear in a heap of this kind. Ground elder and dandelion roots will not disintegrate; they can be put out to wither thoroughly and will be suitable for the main heaps. The resulting compost, though not so rich as that from the main heaps, is good for making up seed boxes and potting mixtures. A refinement is to sow surplus pea and bean seeds or other legumes on a maturing heap in late spring; the tops will provide material for the main heaps and the roots will add nitrogen to the bulk. If trailing marrows or pumpkins are used to provide protection, either for these or main heaps, they should be planted just outside and not on the heaps.

Leaf Mould

Large quantities of dead autumn leaves are best composted separately, and for this purpose an area enclosed by wire netting to prevent them from being blown away is advisable. The initial height of the heap can be 90–120 cm (3–4 ft) when quite firmly packed. Thin layers of soil with lime or limestone dust every few centimetres will help the rotting. The compost preparations are best inserted at the half-way stage as it is not easy to make holes in the completed pile. Here again the local authority may be pleased to use your garden for a dump. Provided the leaves do not come from busy roads there should be no danger from lead contamination: lead fumes keep more or less close to the ground, so the leaves would have grown above the danger level. Even though it will heat up quite well for a while, a pile of leaf mould will take at least a year, more often 18 months, to mature, but the half-rotted mould can be used earlier for mulching.

Use of Compost

No hard and fast rules can be laid down as to when compost is ready to use, when to apply it or how much (or how little!) to put on. Many factors are involved such as the type of soil, the general climate, and the crop to be grown subsequently. In a garden which is being converted from the extensive use of artificial fertilisers and poisons larger amounts than normal would be needed, so it may be necessary to phase the conversion over two or three years. Some useful hints on all these points, and also on the diagnosis and rectifying of faults in the composting process, can be found in the Bio-Dynamic Agricultural Association's Handbook. In any case compost should not be dug in deeply but should be confined to the top seven or eight centimetres (3 ins) of soil because this is where the greatest soil activity occurs. It is merely foolish but not fatal to bury the compost and top soil down to a level where the soil inhabitants do not feel at home; they will just die out and a new population will have to establish itself.

Manure should also be built into heaps and treated like compost, but no lime should be added. Thin layers of compost or soil can assist breakdown.

CHAPTER 8

Crop Rotation, Green Manuring and Mulching

Experience has taught cultivators of the soil that if one particular crop is grown year after year on the same piece of ground, the yield gradually falls, the soil structure deteriorates, and there is a likelihood of increasing trouble from insect depredation, diseases and weeds. It can be shown that the crop has made a drain on particular elements in the soil, and that the micro-life in the soil is altered; furthermore, tests have shown that the soil loses its dynamic quality and assumes a more lifeless condition. Evidence from many countries supports the view that such crops lose nutritional value for humans or animals. On the other hand, if the crop is moved to fresh ground, yields and nutritional value are maintained. Different botanical families make different demands on the nutrients in the soil, so it is sensible to change the crop growing on a particular area of ground in successive years. Putting this principle into practice is known as *crop rotation*. Broadly speaking the gardener is mainly concerned with producing a large assortment of crops—roots, brassicas, peas and beans, salad vegetables and fruit such as tomatoes, marrows and sweet corn. The order in which these are grown on a given patch of land is important.

From years of observation gardeners have found that some crops need a rich soil, if they are to grow well, and a broad generalisation would include in this class the leafy vegetables, leeks, the brassica family, celery and the cucurbita family; they are often referred to as 'heavy feeders' or 'gross feeders'. Traditionally these are the crops that have received heavy dressings of farmyard manure. In contrast we have the 'light feeders', the root-vegetables—carrots, beet, radishes and so on whose flavour is enhanced by a well-matured compost. Finally we have the members of the legume family—the peas and beans which respond to a compost of the leaf-mould type but which also enrich the soil with the nitrogen-collecting bacteria in the nodules on their roots; thus they act as soil improving members of a rotation.

This would suggest that you divide your garden into three plots, feeding them according to the previous paragraph and then planting them with appropriate vegetables. The following year you would change the occupants of the beds, putting the legumes where the heavy feeders had been, the roots where the legumes had been, and the heavy feeding leafy vegetables after the roots, manuring all plots according to the demands of the crop. In the third year the position of the crops would change again, and in the fourth year all crops would return to the beds they occupied in the first year. This is known as a 'three-course rotation'. Home-grown early potatoes are, however, very popular, and the gardener wishing to grow them would have to divide his garden into four plots, thus making a 'four-course rotation' of potatoes, brassicas, legumes and roots.

For a small garden, a simple basic rotation, adaptable to many needs, could be:

1st year: Heavy feeders such as the cabbage family, potatoes, with manure
2nd year: Peas, beans and onions
3rd year: Compost lovers such as beetroot, carrots, spinach, lettuce, etc.

It frequently happens that many gardens cannot conveniently be divided into three or four more or less equal plots, and in such cases one has to fall back on some more flexible arrangement, while still adhering to the basic principle that different types of crop should be moved round year by year. As explained later, it is usually possible to fit fertility-building crops into the main programme, and so to keep the ground covered during gaps: this practice offers an ideal opportunity of giving an extra treatment with preparation 500. Owing to the popularity of the various brassicas one can seldom follow the ideal of leaving three years between them, but at least one clear year, and preferably two, should elapse before returning to them. This arrangement is necessary not only from the soil nutrient point of view, but also to guard against club root attack. The wise gardener will spend a little time each winter making a detailed cropping plan for the coming season and will keep it corrected if alterations have to be made for practical reasons later on. These plans, if carefully filed, provide a very useful record on which to base the next and future plans.

On a somewhat larger scale than the average home garden, here is a suggestion for a longer rotation still, practised and described by its bio-dynamic originator:

Many years ago I decided to have a longer rotation than the usual three- or four-course. There are times with short rotations when ground is occupied by spring greens planted the previous autumn and you are dying to get onto it to sow peas and beans. The solution is to have the spring greens in one bed and the autumn and winter greens in another. The rotation has now become a five-year one. With the inclusion of a fertility-building crop we have a six-course rotation as follows:

1st year: Fertility-building crop (details p. 63)
2nd year: Potatoes (when lifted spring greens are planted out)
3rd year: Spring greens
4th year: Roots
5th year: Autumn and winter greens
6th year: Peas, beans, onions
7th year: Start rotation again with the fertility-building crop

Detailed cropping plans for each plot are not given as different gardeners have different needs and specialities. Salad and quick-growing crops are fitted into gaps in the main plan; vacant ground can usually be found to provide a succession of these important adjuncts to the diet. Onions are included in the legume break because they do not fit in with the root vegetables'

Plot	1st Year	2nd Year	3rd Year	4th Year	5th Year	6th Year
1	Fertility-building crop	Potatoes followed by spring greens	Spring greens	Roots	Autum and winter greens	Peas, beans and onions
2	Potatoes followed by spring greens	Spring greens	Roots	Autumn and winter greens	Peas, beans and onions	Fertility-building crop
3	Spring greens	Roots	Autumn and winter greens	Peas, beans and onions	Fertility-building crop	Potatoes followed by spring greens
4	Roots	Autumn and winter greens	Peas, beans and onions	Fertility-building crop	Potatoes followed by spring greens	Spring greens
5	Autumn and winter greens	Peas, beans and onions	Fertility-building crop	Potatoes followed by spring greens	Spring greens	Roots
6	Peas, beans and onions	Fertility-building crop	Potatoes followed by spring greens	Spring greens	Roots	Autumn and winter greens

more modest requirements. Fruiting vegetables such as sweet corn and members of the marrow family are also included here. It is important to plant the taller-growing peas and beans in rows running north and south; otherwise there will be shading difficulties on the north side.

It will be seen that the above rotation takes leguminous plants round the garden twice if one includes the fertility-building vetches, and the rye straw from the fertility break adds very valuable silica when worked into the soil. The planting timetable is not too intricate, leaving reasonable time between the harvesting of one main crop and the sowing of the next. Such a rotation has the further advantage that the soil will have been called upon to produce leaf crops, root crops, flowers (vetches), and seed or fruit: thus all the forces required for plant growth are being summoned from the various parts of the garden, and there is no one-sided emphasis.

This example has been quoted at some length to illustrate how the important idea of crop rotation can be put into practice bearing bio-dynamic principles in mind. It is not given in a dogmatic way as a scheme which must be followed, but it is intended more as a guide, especially for the newcomer. It is not even all-inclusive—for instance strawberries do not specifically come into it, and yet they have to be moved around in conjunction with other crops. The fact is that crop planning is an individual exercise; no two gardens, however successful they may be, will ever follow exactly the same rotation.

Green Manuring

Mention has already been made of green manuring and fertility-building. Many gardeners will maintain that they cannot afford the space for crops which will not give them an edible or floral return, and yet they will be the first to complain when things start to go wrong owing to declining fertility. But a fertile soil is the first essential towards a flourishing garden, for health in the garden starts with the soil, not with sprays of pesticides and herbicides. It is possible to obtain higher yields from a small area of ground than from a larger area not so well managed. In the six-year rotation described above it will be noticed that one sixth of the garden is given over to fertility-building crops for a whole year. This plot is cultivated in the following way.

In the autumn or early spring the plot is dug or rotavated; then in late February or early March it is given whatever manure or compost can be spared and 500 is sprayed. It is raked or cultivated to form a seed bed and vetches (also known as tares) are sown at the rate of 500 g per 25 sq. m (1 lb per 30 sq. yds), putting the seeds in 3–5 cm (1½-2 in) deep. When signs of flower buds appear 501 is sprayed. In late June the vetches come into flower and are trampled down and broken up. If a rotary mower is available, run it over them. A mixture of dried blood and hoof and horn meal is scattered over the debris, preferably when it is damp, at the rate of 1.5 kg per 25 sq. m (3 lb per 30 sq. yds). It is left to rot for about a week and then chopped into the ground or rotavated in. The bed is raked over after spraying with 500 and rye is sown at about 500 g per 33 sq. m (1 lb per 40 sq. yds). When it is well grown 501 is sprayed. In late autumn (certainly before the end of December) the rye is chopped down and dug in roughly but in such a way that it does not regenerate. The ground is left rough over the winter and is then in first class condition for cultivating before planting the following potato crop in the spring.

Fertility-building crops can, however, be planted over shorter periods, especially if one is attempting to keep the ground covered whenever possible. As the season advances and crops start coming off the land in August and September, there is often nothing to replace them apart from late lettuce, corn salad, radishes and so on, which do not require much room. So in a flexible rotation it is then a sound practice to sow winter tares or rye or a mixture of the two at the rates given above; they will grow all through the winter, albeit slowly, and provide a good bulk of green material for digging in during March or April, by which time they will have put on a spurt. Leave four to six weeks for this material to disintegrate before sowing or planting the next crop; this is a good preparation for brassicas. If, however, the next crop is to be roots, it is often better to cut the green material at ground level and, after allowing it to wilt, put it into the compost heap. The roots of the tares will have added nitrogen to the soil and they break down very quickly, leaving an excellent tilth for sowing.

Other quick-growing crops to fill a gap in the main pro-gramme are agricultural lupins, rape and mustard, but the last two *must not* be planted on land which is subject to club root. Rape is a good collector of potash but is slow to germinate in a cold soil early in the spring; it can, however, be successfully mixed with tares in autumn sowings. Mustard is especially valuable for bee-keepers if sown in August or early September as it provides a late honey flow in October to build up the winter stores. The plants will die back with the first hard frost, if not before, and can be left on the surface to make a dead cover and plenty of worm food. Mustard also, if sown earlier and dug in when the first flowers have opened, is a good remedy on soil which is infested with wireworms. Lupins are usually cut and dug in soon after flowering before the seed has started to develop. As with vetches in the long term, mustard and lupins help to balance the soil by drawing on its potentiality to produce flowers; apart from the peas and beans it does not often get this opportunity in a vegetable garden.

In a town garden where there may be difficulties in obtaining adequate materials for composting, these extra catch crops are especially valuable. In addition to the leafy bulk above the ground the quantity of roots left in the soil is far greater than is usually supposed, and as the rootlets decompose they become a major agent for improving the structure of the soil. Then if leguminous plants have been grown, there is the additional advantage of nitrogen derived from their root nodules.

Mulching

'Mulch' is the term used for a covering put on the surface of the soil to retain moisture, and as a protection against drying winds, hot sunshine and the battering effects of heavy rain; it has the additional purpose of smothering weeds. Judiciously used, mulching is a very valuable practice whether a garden is bio-dynamic or not. In the former case only materials of organic origin are used; newspaper, black polythene and suchlike are not generally recommended. Before applying a mulch make sure that the soil is moist, rake it over lightly and remove any weeds, and then give a spray of 500. To be fully effective a mulch should normally be at least 5–7.5 cm (2–3 in) deep depending on the type of material.

As with composting, there may be difficulties in finding the materials; but there is quite a large choice, though one has to decide whether it might be better to put whatever is available into the compost heap. If, however, mulching has priority, it can be regarded as sheet composting, for the mulch will slowly rot down and be taken into the soil by worms and other soil inhabitants, thus increasing the humus content. In this case it is of advantage to add small quantities of the compost prepara-tions when stirring the 500.

Materials can be very roughly divided into two categories— coarse and not so coarse—and the purposes for which each is used vary slightly. Among the coarser possibilities are straw, bracken and spoilt hay; but it is advisable to make sure that the straw does not come from a field which has been sprayed with herbicide, for some of the poison may persist and damage the mulched crop. Also in spoilt hay there may be grasses which have gone to seed and which therefore would seriously aggravate the weed problem. Dead leaves can be useful in the autumn if they are not required for making leafmould. More especially they can be thickly spread round soft fruit bushes and raspberry rows; they protect the soil against frost, help to retain some of the summer warmth and encourage worms; but they may need to be anchored with a little brushwood or old pea sticks to prevent strong winds from blowing them away. Wood chippings are sometimes suggested as mulch but they break down very slowly and may draw on some of the precious soil nitrogen in the process. There is also a possible danger in that timber is often treated with poisonous fungicides. The same remarks apply to sawdust.

Another purpose of mulching with coarse material is to prevent serious soil compaction where frequent treading cannot be avoided, for instance when harvesting soft fruit or vegetables such as peas and beans or brussels sprouts. When digging over the ground after clearing mulched sprouts, it is quite astonishing to see the number of worms which have been attracted to the crumbling straw.

In the not so coarse category are half-rotted leafmould, grass cuttings, compost and, perhaps best of all, spent hops from a brewery. Unfortunately nowadays breweries are fewer, larger and generally situated in cities. But it is sometimes possible for people with bigger gardens to obtain a load delivered for the cost of the transport. In this case the heap must be left to heat up and mature for at least a month before use. These finer mulches are usually put on in late spring or early summer after the crops have started to grow; they should never be applied to a soil which has not had a chance to warm up, as mulching a cold soil will hinder the warming process and lead to disappointing results. Peat is often used as a fine mulch; but apart from its high cost it has lost any life forces which the original vegetation might have contained, and even the plant nutrient content is remarkably low. Furthermore, strict conservationists might object to its use on the grounds that it is a non-renewable resource!

Mulching is of course the basis of what is known as the 'no-dig' system; but in the absence of personal experience it would be imprudent to comment on the method.

CHAPTER 9

Cultivations

This is a very elementary chapter in which are discussed the various operations and tools that are necessary to prepare the soil in readiness for sowing seeds or for receiving young plants; the subsequent cultivation of established crops is also included. It must be recognised at the outset that there can be no hard and fast rules; the methods chosen will depend upon soil type, the crop to be grown, the time of year, and personal preferences derived from experience. There is, however, one guiding princi-ple to be observed as far as possible and that is to avoid burying the top 5–7.5 cm (2–3 in) of soil because, as explained in Chapter 3, here dwell most of the active micro-organisms which endow the soil with life: if they are transferred to an unfriendly environment lower down, they will die out and a new population has to become established before full fertility can be restored. Another consideration is to maintain, and where necessary improve, the structure of the soil.

NEW GARDENS

It may be as well to begin by considering the problems present-ing themselves when starting a new garden from a meadow, neglected land or a battered building site. Whatever the con-ditions it is advisable at an early stage to draw up a plan in-corporating the main features of the garden it is hoped to create. Among other things these might include paths, the vegetable patch, the composting area, the herbaceous borders, lawns and the sites for top or bush fruit. In choosing a place for a greenhouse one needs a southern aspect, easy access and proximity to the main electricity supply. If the garden is on a slope, be careful not to plan for hedges against which cold air, flowing down the hill, might accumulate to form a frost pocket; on the other hand a stout hedge at the top end of the plot can arrest such a flow and divert it elsewhere. In particular peg out the lines of proposed paths; it may be possible to leave them for later attention, and in the meanwhile they will provide access to the other parts of the plot without the disadvantage of consolidating newly treated land.

In the case of meadow land there are two possibilities—either to skim off the turf with 2–3 cm (1 in) or so of soil and stack it to break down into a potting compost with the assistance of the compost preparations, or to turn everything in after cutting off any long growth for compost. The choice will largely depend on the amount of perennial weed present such as couch grass, buttercups, docks, thistles and so on. If they preponderate, it is probably better to skim, using a turfing iron, spade or rotavator, and then to fork over the bared ground to remove tap roots. Long tap roots are best tackled with a spade. Drive it in about 2.5 cm (1 in) from the top of the root and gently push the handle backwards without inverting the sod; the leverage of the end of the spade against the root will usually loosen the roothold lower down and the whole root can be pulled out by hand. Roots up to 45 cm (18 in) long may be extracted in this way. A lot of future trouble is avoided by doing this job thoroughly. After removing as many perennial weed roots as possible, spray the loosely worked soil with 500 to which small amounts of the compost preparation may be added before stirring. Then, if the job has been done in early autumn, give a light dressing of compost and sow with rye or winter tares and rape for digging in during the spring. On the other hand, if the soil is on the heavy side it may be preferable to work it into ridges about 23 cm (9 in) high and expose it to the action of winter frosts which will make it friable for spring sowings.

If the job has been done in the spring and there is no special hurry to produce flowers or vegetables, a green manure crop of lupins or vetches perhaps mixed with rape can be grown, again with some compost. This can be worked in during the summer before planting with brassicas, leeks, celeriac and so on, which have been brought on separately. If, however, there is an urgent need for vegetables, a heavy dressing of compost or manure must be given and in this case the addition of the compost preparations to the 500 becomes a must.

If it has been decided to incorporate the turf rather than skim it, the best time is the autumn. The turf is cut into smallish clods about 7.5 cm (3 in) deep which are then built top downwards to form ridges up to 30 cm (1 ft) high and 90 cm (3 ft) from centre to centre. Preparation 500 plus the compost preparations can be sprayed either before or after this operation. During the winter and early spring the turf should have broken down sufficiently for potatoes to be planted directly in the ridges. The haulm will help to smother out most of the weeds and those germinating in the troughs can be controlled by further earthing up. During or after harvest the ground is levelled and the usual winter green manure crops are sown. An alternative is to work some compost into the troughs before harvest and plant brassicas for winter and spring use. Spreading the ridges around the already established plants during harvest will help the brassicas and will anchor sprouts and sprouting broccoli which are so liable to be rocked by the wind. Before adopting this method, however, it is advisable to make sure that the turf is not infested with wireworms. These are larvae of the click beetle; they are tough, white to golden, rather thin creatures, up to 2.5 cm (1 in) long. They take up to four years to develop fully and are particularly fond of potatoes. If they are present the best plan is to invert the clods of turf and expose them to starlings or other birds for a fortnight before stacking them. Then sow a crop of mustard to be dug in when it starts to flower; this is an old effective remedy against wireworms.

Bringing neglected gardens or derelict land back into use is a laborious task and on larger areas it may be necessary to hire mechanical equipment; in this case persuade the operator not to bring any of the subsoil up to the surface. Another possibility for a large garden might be to get in a gang of 'Woofers'. (WOOF is an organisation which provides opportunities for town dwellers to spend weekends on organic farms and gardens doing special jobs in return for food and shelter).

As a rule neglected land will either be covered with brambles, saplings and nettles, or it will have deteriorated to a mat of perennial weeds which may consist of creeping grasses, rosebay willowherb, creeping thistle, coltsfoot and ground elder, with dandelions and docks thrown in for good measure! The soil under the former cover is likely to be more fertile and in better tilth than the latter. There are two major types of creeping grasses, both of which are difficult to eradicate completely: they have various local names which are sometimes interchanged. One species is *Agropyron repens*, commonly known as couch grass, squitch or twitch. Its creeping stems are comparatively fleshy, but those which go down deeper are thinner. It does not flower very profusely and the spikelets are borne alternately close to the stem like rye grass. The other invader is *Agrostis tenuis*, the common bent. Its leaves and creeping stems are much more slender than couch and this makes it more difficult to eradicate. It flowers freely, bearing open feathery heads on thin stalks.

The first step in tackling a nettle/bramble complex is to clear the top growth, chopping any soft material into short lengths with a sharp spade for composting, and consigning the coarser stuff to the bonfire. Grubbing out the roots can be done with some kind of mattock or pickaxe, but an Assam or Chillington fork is a better tool though not so well known; it is a stout three-pronged implement mounted at right angles to the haft. As soon as a sizeable area has been cleared, spray 500 and cultivate for a green manure crop appropriate to the time of the year; there should be enough residual fertility for this to become well established. A perennial mat will need different treatment. In late spring or summer it will probably be worthwhile to scythe off the top growth for composting. Then one can adopt the skimming method described for pasture land, in which case a Chillington hoe is a tool well worth trying. The other alternative, apart from rotavating, is steadily to work through the area with a garden fork, removing as many roots as possible by hand. There is no need to shake out all the earth from tufts of couch and other weeds; they, together with the other roots, can be built into a long-term compost heap (see Chapter 7). The other possibility is to rotavate the plot, with or without skimming.

This is best started in spring and will have to be repeated several times. The first run will merely chop up the roots into small pieces, each of which will produce a new plant. But if the operation is repeated as soon as the ground appears green, the bits of roots will have lost some of their food reserves when producing the new shoots, so that the next batch of shoots will be weaker. Eventually, after four or five runs, all the bits will have died from exhaustion. The plot will then be ready, after spraying 500, to take a green manure crop or to be brought into production; in the latter case it will need a good dressing of compost or manure.

If he or she is lucky, the owner of a new house when starting to make a garden will be faced with one of the situations already described, but there may be additional problems. Although building contractors are supposed to pile separately any topsoil and subsoil moved during their operations, this is a counsel of perfection not often found in practice. Things will be even worse if heavy earthmoving equipment has been used to level the site and dig channels for drains. The first thing of course is to remove any builders' debris and rubble. On heavy land it may then be advisable to put in some tile drains provided that there is sufficient slope and a convenient outlet for them. Drainage can also be effected by burying rubble in trenches 30 cm (1 ft) wide and at least 45 cm (18 in) deep, but again there must be a suitable outlet for the surplus water. Drainage, if considered necessary and practicable, must be completed before any other work is attempted.

The next step, after making a plan, is to examine the subsoil position. If no more than 2.5 cm (1 in) or so has been spread over the original topsoil, it can be incorporated when preparing the land. But if several centimetres have been dumped over an appreciable area, one solution would be to double trench it, putting the subsoil down where it belongs. Another way is to try and convert the subsoil into topsoil; the following method would also apply to subsoil which has been completely exposed. Spread any topsoil which may be available over the surface, together with 5 cm (2 in) of manure or commercial compost and broadcast mustard seed, working it in lightly after spraying 500. Turn it in when it reaches the flowering stage and repeat the process, allowing a week or two for the first lot to rot down. The second or third crop could well be a legume—lupins or winter tares according to the season.

A few words about rotavators may not come amiss at this stage. First, the question must be asked: is it a desirable tool for *my* garden? Some acquaintance with the general principles of the internal combustion engine is essential; it is time-consuming and expensive to go round to the nearest garage every time the thing fails to start or loses power. For gardens of less than ¼ acre (1,000 square metres) mechanical aid is not usually necessary; even the smallest machines are somewhat unwieldy and require space for turning, possibly interfering with growing crops. In fact one uses almost as much time and physical energy man-oeuvring a machine on a small job as one would if doing it by hand!

There are two main types on the market—those with wheels and those without. Machines with wheels propel themselves and merely have to be steered, but they have been known to get out of control by an inexperienced operator when turning at the end of a run. They are usually adapted to take a tool bar for weeding and, more useful still, a ridging tool. On the other hand, although adjustable, they cultivate at constant depths and the action of the blades is liable to create a pan on heavy or poorer types of soil. On a flinty clay or gardens where rubble has been dumped in the past, flints or bits of brick and cement can cause irritating delays by jamming between the blades and the shield. Machines without wheels have the advantage that depth of cultivation can be easily varied, and they are not so liable to blockage by large stones; but they are as a rule not adaptable for jobs other than preliminary cultivations. When either type of machine is being used to incorporate a green manure crop, it is essential to ensure that the blades are sharp enough to chop it up—otherwise the stems will clog things up.

Trenching

The conventional methods of deep digging, trenching and double trenching are not as a general rule recommended, not because they do not work but because they are so often unnecessary. The main exception to this observation is a heavy clay soil on which it may occasionally be advisable to loosen the subsoil by double trenching in order to improve root penetration and drainage. Shallow trenching is, however, a useful way of incorporating green manure. In this case take out a trench not more than 10 cm (4 in) deep and a spade's width across the plot, and cart the spoil to the other end. With the spade remove the material from the next spit and chop it up in the trench; then turn the cleared soil, roots uppermost, onto the chopped material, thus making the next trench. If a little compost or manure is available for mixing with the greenery, it will hasten the rotting and at the same time will confer the benefits of the compost preparations. The final trench is filled with the soil taken out at the start. The land must now be left for up to a month before sowing or planting, depending on the time of the year and the warmth of the soil. The micro-life working on the green material makes a heavy demand on the soil nitrogen in the early stages, and any crop planted at this time will be starved. But once this stage of decomposition is completed the nitrogen will again become available, together with the extra amount derived from the green crop. Also remember that the micro-life needs air, so compaction of the surface after trenching must be avoided at all costs.

PREPARATION OF SEED BEDS

The chief objective when preparing land for sowing is to create a fine tilth which will allow free access of air and not be so loose and puffy that the capillary action of the soil water is disturbed. Any cavities in the soil left after rough digging must be eliminated. The work should be done on a dry day when the soil is moist but not so moist that it sticks to the tools. However urgent the job may seem, it can be disastrous to try and work a wet soil—it will coagulate into small lumps which the air cannot penetrate and which will be difficult to break up later on. Impatience can often prove to be the worst enemy of the gardener. A heavy soil which has dried out into hard clods may present difficulties if there is no prospect of early rain; in this case the use of a hose can be very beneficial. The ground is sprayed evenly with moderately sized droplets until the water has really penetrated the clods and is then left for two or three hours to dry out a little before breaking them down. If the watering has been well done, it is quite remarkable how easily the clods will crumble. Generally speaking it is advisable to work the soil to a depth of 5–7.5 cm (2–3 in) without inverting it. If small seeds are to be sown, a finer tilth is needed than for large seeds or if the bed is being prepared for transplanting seedlings. For those who try to work with the rhythms of the moon it is necessary to time the final cultivation carefully.

On non-mechanised gardens the usual tool for creating a seed bed is a rake, but this is not altogether satisfactory. On the average type of rake the teeth are not long enough to penetrate to the desired depth, and they are too close together to run easily through the soil. A better tool for the initial stages is some kind of cultivator with arrowhead tynes on prongs curved in such a way that they are parallel with the surface when the tool is pulled through the soil. There are several types on the market, some with three tynes, some with five; those with arrows at least 2.5 cm (1 in) wide at the base are to be preferred. It is often possible to use this tool instead of digging or rotavating a plot which is carrying only a light cover of weeds.

The final smoothing off of the seed bed is done with a rake which will collect any stones and weeds loosened by the cultivator. Preparation 500 can usefully be sprayed just before or just after the first cultivation, but this application may be postponed until after the seed has been sown provided that the soil is sufficiently moist to absorb the droplets thoroughly; remember that 500 is most effective when sprayed in late afternoon or in the evening. If a rotavator is used to prepare a seed bed, it is essential to control the depth of cultivation very carefully; restrict the action to not more than 7.5 cm (3 in), preferably rather less. Rotavation is liable to leave the soil in too puffy condition so it is advisable to find some means of consolidation. On a farm scale this would be done with a fluted (Cambridge) roller; but in a garden gentle treading followed by a very shallow raking may be the best solution. Alternatively, the soil will settle down naturally if left for a week or two. The point to note is that germination failures or delays can often be traced to puffiness in the seed bed.

Pelleted Seed

A comparatively recent practice of most seedsmen is to coat some of their smaller seeds with clay, forming little pellets which are easier to handle. Each pellet contains one seed only, enabling sowing to be done much more thinly and reducing the work of final spacing. The clay may be 'fortified' with insecticide, fungicide and/or soluble fertiliser. Even if one is prepared to accept the additions, experience with pellets is varied. Like the little girl, 'when they are good, they are very very good, but when they are bad they are horrid.' The critical factor is soil moisture. If the seed bed is on the dry side, the moisture cannot fully penetrate the clay coating even though an uncoated seed would be able to germinate in those conditions. In wet conditions the pellets are liable to become a mess, giving the seeds a tendency to rot.

A still more recent innovation is to pregerminate ('chit') the seed on damp cloth or blotting paper. As soon as the rootlets break through the seed coats the seeds are mixed into a gelatinous paste which is then put into a pliable container with some kind of a nozzle—a polythene bag with one corner snipped off will serve the purpose. Single seeds can then be gently squeezed out through the nozzle along the drill. In this way it is possible to get an even distribution of seed at any desired spacing with the assurance that growth has already started. For those who adhere strictly to the moon rhythms it should be noted that these effects work via the soil, so seed to be sown by this method must be put to 'chit' beforehand; two to three days will generally be sufficient for most small seeds in warm conditions, but it may be advisable to do a preliminary test in advance.

Once the seeds have germinated there are two main objectives to be borne in mind. The first is to keep weeds under control and above all to prevent them from seeding. The second is to prevent a crust from forming on the top of the soil, or if it has formed to break it up as soon as possible. Both objectives can be achieved simultaneously by hoeing or, as already described, by mulching. There are several different types of hoe available and it is useful to have two, one operated by a dragging action and the other by pushing. The aim is to work as close as possible to the seedlings without damaging them and to cut off all the weeds just below ground level. It is usually better to work backwards so that all footmarks are loosened and the weeds are not given a second chance by being trodden back into the soil.

Thinning

The next job is to thin out the seedlings to the desired spacing. This is best done when they have made three or four true leaves and have not begun to crowd one another out too severely. The work can often be started roughly with a hoe and very skilful gardeners can even do the final 'singling' in this way; but for the average person the final selection of the strongest seedling more or less in the right place is best done by hand. With some crops it is possible to fill any gaps by transplanting unwanted strong seedlings but they need to be lifted carefully for this purpose. Beetroot is a case in point.

Transplanting

The best time to transplant is the afternoon or evening during a period of descending moon, even if the plants have been raised individually in pots or seed blocks. When seedlings are being taken from seed beds it is quite a good plan to lift them in the morning while the upward expanding forces are at their strongest and to put them away in a cool shady place until later. Their roots may profitably be put into a receptacle containing stirred 500 or a dilute solution of liquid manure (preferably cow). Cowdung and more particularly its urine normally contains some indolyl acetic acid—a root-promoting hormone—in its natural form; in synthetic form it is marketed under various trade names for treating cuttings.

The tilth on the plot to be planted up need not be so fine as that for a seed bed unless very tender seedlings such as lettuce or some annual flowers are being moved. On soils which easily become compacted it may be advisable to use a long plank for standing on; this distributes one's weight evenly over a large area and a subsequent light hoeing quickly restores the tilth. Mark out the planting stations before starting the planting. Make the holes large enough for the roots to be spread out, and deep enough to take the tap root (if any) without bending it upwards. With plants from individual pots be sure to spread out the network of roots that will have formed round the sides and bottom. Press the soil gently but firmly round the roots, and give each plant a little tug to make sure that it is properly anchored. A little fine, well rotted compost in each hole will help the plants to get established quickly.

A useful dibber for making planting holes can be made by cutting down and bluntly pointing the handle of an old spade or fork. After using such a tool it is absolutely essential to ensure that the bottoms of the holes have been thoroughly filled when planting; if a small pocket of air is left beneath it, a plant gets 'hung' and will not thrive.

RAISING SEEDLINGS

Many flowers and vegetables cannot usefully be sown in their final places in the garden because of frost damage, initial overcrowding, and getting land ready in time. So the seeds are germinated and brought on by various methods in a greenhouse, cold frame, or under some other form of protection. The alternative is, later on, to buy in seedlings all ready to plant out; but such young plants will not have the potential vigour or disease resistance of those raised bio-dynamically, and one loses the satisfaction of doing the job oneself, thereby establishing a personal relationship with the plants right from the start.

The first consideration is to prepare a suitable growth medium for the seedlings. Various composts (in the other sense of the word) are available commercially, but most of them are 'fortified' with substances which are not altogether desirable from the bio-dynamic point of view, and again it is more satisfying to prepare one's own mixtures. The main desiderata are plenty of mature humus, an open texture to provide aeration and drainage, and a capacity to retain moisture. A good formula for germination which does not need to be very rich is:

2 parts fibrous loam or long term compost (see p. 57)
1 part granulated peat or fine leafmould
2 parts grit or coarse sand

The ingredients are thoroughly mixed up and left ready for use in a heap, protected from heavy rain. When 500 is being used elsewhere in the garden, spare a little to spray on the heap.

When the seedlings have germinated and are just large enough to handle conveniently, they need a richer mixture in the containers to which they are moved, and the formula is changed to:

2 parts grit or coarse sand
3 parts granulated peat or leafmould
7 parts loam or long term compost

with a scattering of hoof and horn, bone meal and limestone dust. To this, varying amounts of fully mature rich compost are added according to the species being handled. Tomatoes, peppers and celeriac are the most demanding, but flower bedding plants and the marrow family are not so greedy.

One snag is that loam and most composts contain weed seeds. One can put up with them, but it is possible to sterilise small quantities in a colander or gauze container placed over a pan of boiling water. Sterilisation in a large open pan over a fire is not recommended as it is impossible to control the temperature at a level which will not damage the humus. Another way is to spread out the compost thinly, keeping it moist enough for the seeds to germinate, and then let them wither by withholding water.

The different types of container—pots, seed boxes and so on—are nowadays so numerous that they cannot be described in detail here. But there is a DIY way worthy of mention: it is to make your own soil blocks and dispense with pots, and even boxes, altogether. The second compost formula above is used, but a little practice is necessary to gauge the right consistency—sufficiently firm to prevent crumbling, but open enough for the plant roots to penetrate. Each seedling is put into the compost just before the last stage of compaction. Once the seedling has started to grow its roots help to keep the block firm, and when they begin to peep through the sides, the plant is ready to go out just as it is into its final position. This method has advantages over the type of pot which disintegrates when placed in the soil (and often before that!), for the disintegration of the latter can be irregular and the material may contain undesirable substances. It also avoids the formation of a mass of roots coiled round the bottom of the more usual plastic or clay pots.

Watering seedlings in pots and boxes sometimes presents problems. Very often the compost at the bottom dries out and water applied to the surface runs straight through without moistening the dry parts; the sides and corners of boxes are apt to suffer from this fault. If there is a suspicion that this is happening it can easily be remedied by standing the containers in a pan of water for 20 minutes or so. The best answer is to prevent the trouble by putting the containers in direct contact with the soil, or else on a bed of coarse grit which can be kept thoroughly moistened. Seedlings in soil blocks need to be watered regularly by a fine spray from above.

Sometimes seedlings in boxes and trays fall flat and die soon after germination. The phenomenon is known as 'damping off', and a close examination will show that the stems have rotted at the base. It is due to a fungus which appears when conditions are too wet and there is a lack of air in the soil. The fault may be caused by overwatering or by an insufficiently porous compost mixture; poor ventilation can be a contributory cause. Occasionally it is possible to save some of the still sound seedlings by taking them from the infected container, washing them and then pricking them out into a more open-textured medium.

CHAPTER 10

Weeds

by B. Saunders-Davies

Bio-dynamic growers are often asked what they do about weeds. For the farmer, working on a large scale, it is even more of a problem than it is for the gardener. In a vegetable garden most is done by hoeing and hand weeding. For some crops a flame gun can be helpful when weeds germinate before the crop and can be burned off. This sometimes works with carrots, but the weather may prevent the use of the flame gun in the few days available. Some weeds are indicators of soil conditions or faulty cultivations. Some are favourable companion plants and some, such as poppies in cornfields, are bad. Animal remains like bones, feathers, wool, blood and meals made from them encourage weeds if used directly on the soil. They should be thoroughly composted with other vegetable material and used as mature compost.

A useful hint from Maria Thun, which many people, especially farmers, have found helpful, is to cultivate the soil when the sun is in the constellation of the Lion (mid-August to mid-September), when the greatest numbers of annual weeds of many varieties will germinate. They can then be ploughed or dug in before the next crop is sown.

Ashes

Rudolf Steiner described another way of tackling weeds if they become really troublesome. The moon is connected with reproductive forces and has an effect on germination and growth. It works through the watery element and is therefore stronger in wet years. We must make the soil unsuitable to support those lunar forces, for if we can prevent the Moon exerting its effect, the reproductive capacity of the weed will be hindered. The opponent of the weed is fire and the reproductive force of the weed is in its seed, so if the seed is burned, the reproductive forces are hindered. A certain quantity of the particular seed is gathered and burned in a wood fire or stove and the ashes scattered lightly over the weedy area. A large quantity is not required since the effect radiates, but it may be advisable to repeat the ash treatment in a month's time. There is a cycle of four years with many things in nature, so if we persist in scattering the ashes, the reproductive power of the seed will be weakened in the second year. By the third year it should have lost its viability so that in the fourth year there should be very few surviving. Some people have had very good results with docks, for instance, after four years, but not everyone is always successful. More research is needed to determine what other influences may be involved.

Weed Brew

A sort of liquid brew can also be made from weeds. Put a quantity into a barrel or bucket of water. Stir occasionally and when the plant material is completely decomposed the liquid can be sprayed where the weeds are troublesome. It should be sprayed three times when the Moon is in the Crab and repeated the following month and the next if necessary. This is especially suitable for the runners and roots of creeping and climbing weeds. It is usually effective but can be disappointing owing to unforeseen circumstances.

Maria Thun has been doing practical research for 40 years on the effects of the Moon and the constellations on plant growth, weeds, insect and animal pests. She has found that certain homoeopathic potencies of the ashes are more effective than the plain ashes. This work is described in detail in her booklet, *Weed and Pest Control. Based on Research into the Effects of Constellations and Potencies*.

CHAPTER 11

Plant Diseases

Strictly speaking, plants do not suffer from diseases in the same way as animals and human beings; the troubles usually classified as diseases are to be seen more as malfunctions which appear when soil and/or climatic conditions become favourable for the development of fungi or bacteria. (Viruses, as explained later, fall into a rather different category.) A great deal of such trouble can be prevented by cultural practices, by the choice of resistant seed varieties and by careful observation. This is not surprising in view of what has already been said about the very intimate connections between soil and plant: adverse conditions in the soil will inevitably be reflected in the plants growing on it. Two major soil factors can be responsible for the appearance of fungus diseases on plants—poor drainage or compaction, and the use of manure in too raw a state. In the former case the fungal activity, whose proper place is in the soil and the compost heap, is restricted by lack of air; to compensate for this imbalance a similar activity in different form starts up in the plants. In the latter case the plants are forced to take up too much water, to grow too lushly as if being fed on soluble artificial fertilisers; they may also absorb organic substances which have been incompletely transformed. In both cases the life forces of the plants are weakened.

Fungus diseases usually start from tiny spores which may be wind borne or else have been lying around from previous years in litter or in the soil itself. (There is, however, a school of thought which believes that a disease can arise spontaneously under certain circumstances.) A spore does not necessarily infect a plant when it lands on it, even if it finds an encouraging drop of water in which to germinate. A great deal of conventional research has been done to investigate the factors involved in disease resistance. On the one hand it has been found that some kinds of plants contain substances which kill the spores as soon as they penetrate the plant tissues; one such substance has been manufactured artificially and can be sprayed on the foliage as a 'systemic fungicide' in special cases (but it would be sounder to try to discover the conditions under which the plant could be encouraged of itself to produce the substances). On the other hand, there is a natural colonisation of plant leaves by non-pathogenic microbes and yeasts whose function is to prey on developing disease spores, but they are either destroyed or inactivated by standard fungicides. Healthy plants growing in a healthy soil probably achieve both these devices.

Fungi have a great potentiality for very rapid growth and their hyphae—fine hairs (Greek *huphe* = a web)—produce vast numbers of spores; they are therefore strongly influenced by the moon which stimulates both vegetative and procreative reproduction. These moon forces work through the watery element, and Rudolf Steiner implies that they can sometimes work too strongly, creating a superabundance of reproductive activity, and it is on this surplus that a fungus thrives. (For full details see Rudolf Steiner's *Agriculture*, p. 109).

There are other factors that can favour the growth of parasitic fungi. For instance, exotic species growing under conditions other than those prevailing in the places where they evolved are more likely to have their natural balances disturbed in a strange place and so have less resistance. Again there is a seasonal effect. Plants grown out of their normal season are often very difficult to protect against disease because they are subjected to alien rhythms; winter lettuce is a case in point. It is also quite remarkable how the common ephemeral weeds, such as groundsel and shepherd's purse, can be almost shrivelled up by rust from August onwards, even though they have been vigorous all through the spring and summer. Perhaps the declining day length or the movement of the sun into the Lion has stopped the development of a resistance-bestowing factor. This time of year, however, is that in which most of the mushrooms and toadstools produce their reproductive organs.

A slight argument in favour of the spontaneous creation theory mentioned above is the fact that many plant diseases are specific—that is to say that wheat rusts will not attack cabbages, nor will potato blight affect dahlias although it does trouble other members of the Solanaceae. Originally a disease must have started as plant tissue began to break down, though some may aver that the first spores arrived in the dust of comets!

So far we have been mainly concerned with troubles on parts of plants above the ground. Occasionally roots may become affected but root diseases are comparatively rare in any kind of garden, apart from club root in brassicas and one or two others which will be described under specific crops. In a bio-dynamic garden the situation should be kept under control by preparation 505 working through the compost. There is however one nonspecific fungus, *Armillaria mellea*, also known as the honey fungus, which may kill shrubs and trees. Once it has made a kill it is extremely difficult to eliminate as it can lie around for years in old pieces of root which will be missed by even the most careful digging over. If this trouble does occur the area should be grassed over or planted with annuals for some time before replanting with fruit trees or shrubs.

To combat and ward off fungus diseases in general a tea made from *Equisetum arvense* (Common Horsetail) is used. This is not a fungicide in the usual sense of the word; it might better be described as a fungifuge as it counteracts the influences tending to favour fungus development. The dried fronds of the plant are known as Preparation 508. Bring to the boil 20 g (¾ oz or one unit) of the preparation in about a litre (2 pints) of rainwater, and allow to simmer for 20–30 minutes with the lid on, and then let it stand for 24 hours. Strain and add sufficient water to make 4.5 litres (1 gallon). For use, stir for 10–15 minutes as described for 500, and spray as a fine mist on both upper and lower surfaces of the leaves until they are well covered: the soil also should receive some of the spray. The time to spray is when hot, humid or changeable weather conditions are conducive to fungus development on susceptible species. Routine spraying at 10–14 day intervals can be practised against such common

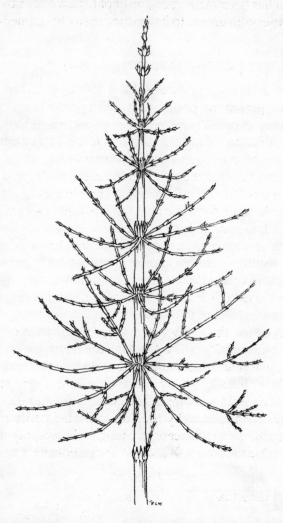

Common Horsetail (*Equisetum arvense*). Preparation 508. *Drawing*:
Tabitha Parsons

diseases as blackspot on roses or botrytis on strawberries,
starting early in the season. Later sprayings can be more
dilute—that is, the original litre can be diluted to 9 litres (2
gallons) and subsequently to as much as 45 litres (10 gallons),
but the solution should always have a pale/yellow-green or
brown colour and should smell of equisetum. Once the original

decoction has been made it can be kept for a week or two, and it is sometimes convenient to have some ready for immediate use.

Fungal Diseases (*by B. Saunders-Davies*)

Fungi are a 'fruiting process'. The mushroom cap we eat is a fruit. The proper place for mushrooms and fungi is in the ground; they are even beneficial in grassland where they provide an outlet for certain superfluous moon forces in the soil and also attract harmful bacteria away from other crops. But if weather and soil conditions are too moist or if full moon and perigee (moon nearest to the earth) occur close together, the moon forces can become too strong and the 'fruiting process' can rise up to a higher level above the ground and cause fungal attack on leaves, fruit and so on. It must be driven back to the ground level where it belongs. These dangers can often be anticipated and preventative action taken. Hoeing in the morning to encourage the outbreathing of the soil can sometimes prevent fungal attack in wet weather.

Above all, use the equisetum tea as a spray on leaves and soil as a preventative. The silica forces in the equisetum counteract the excessive moon forces and drive the fungi forces back to their rightful place. The equisetum tea is best sprayed in the evening. The next morning it is advisable to stimulate the sap circulation of the plants by spraying a diluted nettle tonic (see p. 93) on the soil. If necessary, repeat these sprayings three times (see Maria Thun's *Weed and Pest Control*).

Bacterial Diseases

Bacteria belong to a lower order of life than the fungi. A bacterium is an extremely small creature consisting of only one cell which can only be studied under a powerful microscope. It multiplies by dividing itself into two, and under favourable conditions populations running into millions can build up very rapidly by this method. Beneficial bacteria are important agents in the breakdown of a compost heap. When their work is done or when conditions become adverse they develop a dormant state to await better times. Some species of bacteria are anaerobic, deriving the oxygen they need from the substances on which they are acting; among these are the species which cause putrefaction.

The bio-dynamic gardener should have no cause to worry about bacterial disease. It usually takes the form of wilting due to the bacteria damaging and blocking the water-carrying tubes, but a plant has to reach a very weakened state before this can happen. If it does occur there is not much to be done about it except to remove the plant at once and to cheer up its neighbours with an aerating cultivation and perhaps a foliar spray. In the vegetable garden an occasional pea or bean plant may wilt and die from bacterial attack: the most likely cause is a wound made by the hoe through which the bacteria can gain an entrance.

Virus Diseases

Although virus diseases have probably been in existence for a very long time, it is only in this century that they have assumed importance, perhaps because many strains of both food crops and ornamentals appear to be losing their vigour. Those who attended Rudolf Steiner's lectures on agriculture do not seem to have been worried by viruses for there is no mention of them either in the main lectures or in the questions which followed them.

There is some controversy as to whether viruses are living things in their own right: they are certainly much smaller even than a bacterium and do not have many of the properties of a living cell. Possibly changes in the environment, sensible or supersensible, or weaknesses in the host may bring them into action. Their effects often show up as pale streaks in leaves, and the stripes in some of the most popular tulip flowers are due to a virus. But they can be much more devastating, producing stunted leaves, distortions and shrivelling, as for instance in tomato mosaic disease.

Viruses may be transmitted from plant to plant by sucking insects, usually aphids, and once an aphis has been infected it passes on the infection to its offspring. It is still not certain whether a plant attacked by an infected carrier will inevitably develop the symptoms, or whether really healthy plants have some form of resistance. There is at present no known way of healing a plant once a virus has become active in it. All that can be done is to remove infected plants and put them into the compost heap where they will disintegrate with all their troubles. It is, however, advisable not to replant soft fruit, especially raspberries or strawberries, on land where infected plants have been growing.

Deficiency Diseases

The symptoms of this class of diseases can be rather similar to those of mild virus attack, but the cause, as their name implies, is a shortage of one or more of the chemical elements essential to plant growth. They manifest usually in somewhat smaller leaves which develop coloured patches in the blades or discolouration in the veins and leaf edges; effects may also occur in flower and fruit. Each deficiency, whether of a major or minor element, has its characteristic pattern, and these have all been classified for the benefit of conventional farmers and gardeners. Such troubles generally arise from monocropping or the excessive use of artificial fertilisers with a consequent deterioration in the soil humus. So here again the bio-dynamic gardener need not worry about them unless he or she is struggling with a particularly difficult type of soil. If this kind of trouble is suspected it is best to have it confirmed by an expert. A foliar seaweed spray will often clear things up.

Nematodes or Eelworms

Unthriftiness in plants showing up as reduced growth and severe yellowing of the leaves may sometimes be caused by nematodes or eelworms. Although they look like worms and have some characteristics in common with true worms, they are extremely small creatures only just visible to the naked eye. Their mode of action is to steal most of the nitrogen absorbed by the host's roots before it can reach the stems and leaves.

There are several different kinds, but they are all specific, like most of the fungi. Most of them work in the soil and their cysts can stay dormant for some years, waiting to be awakened by the next planting of the crop on which they thrive. It has been claimed that the root secretions of some plants, *Tagetes patula* in particular, can awaken the cysts which then, not finding the plant of their choice, starve and die. The most likely plants to suffer in the vegetable garden are tomatoes and potatoes, but strawberries may also be affected. In the former cases the small warty swellings on the roots are easily recognised. The safest thing to do is to take up the plants carefully and burn them, for although there are some fungi which can attack the worms there is a danger that the cysts might survive in the compost heap. If a comparatively large area is affected, it would be worth while to try Tagetes[1], as the method of burning the worms, described on p. 94, would be extremely tedious to apply in a garden.

---

1 Tagetes seed and the way to use it can usually be obtained from the Henry Doubleday Research Association, Ryton-on-Dunsmore, Coventry.

CHAPTER 12
Insects and Insect Pests

There are many thousands of different insect species but only a very tiny portion of them can become pests or nuisances to the farmer or gardener. Most of them have their own niches in the great cycles of growth, decay and regeneration which form the milieu of life in our earthly biosphere: the disappearance of even one species would have a marked effect on the ecology of the habitat of which it has become a part. If in our gardens we are to get beyond the 'here's an insect, how can we kill it?' attitude and adopt a more holistic approach, one of the first steps is to discover the extraordinarily close relationship between the plant and insect kingdoms. It almost seems that, in the very earliest evolutionary times, a single archetype or creationary urge divided into two parts; one part descended right down into the earth and became plant while the other hovered above it and became insect. In the highest forms it is not difficult to appreciate the close connection between the seed-leaf-bud-flower sequence of the plant and the egg-larva-pupa-imago sequence of the butterfly: this could be exemplified by the relationship between the tortoiseshell butterfly and the nettle in which the nettle seems to sacrifice the potential colour of its flowers to the perfection of colour in the butterfly. Similar relationships can be traced right down through the lower orders of both kingdoms. And here, be it remarked, the amazing adaptations of floral structures to suit certain insects and the corresponding forms of the insects themselves are not due to some Darwinian mechanism, but have been inherent in the species concerned from the very beginning and have been developed side by side: each is part of the other.

So in our aim to try and work in the garden with nature as a whole, we must be prepared for and even rejoice in the presence of *some* insects on our crops. This will ensure the continuation of nature's intricate network in which every species, be it plant, insect or animal, after attaining fulfilment sacrifices itself and becomes the ground on which another can develop. For instance, the ladybirds and hoverflies are unable to live directly on plants: they need plant sap which has been partially transformed in the bodies of aphids, and this might be seen as the 'purpose' of the aphids. Or again, some species of small wasp can only pass through their larval (growth) stages when nourished by leaf substance which is being digested by caterpillars or other insect types, so they pass this stage in the bodies of their unfortunate, unwilling hosts.

Now it may happen that, through some human action or some imbalance in the weather or the environment, conditions are created which are conducive to the rapid proliferation of one or another insect species. For instance a number of hard air frosts in February and March will delay the emergence of aphids from hibernation but the accompanying sunshine may tempt the ladybirds to come out: finding no nourishment they perish and so the aphids when they all emerge together have nothing to control them and it may take some time for the predator population to build up. In order to save a crop it may then be necessary to use an insecticide, but always give the predators a chance before taking such action. On the other hand, perhaps the gardener himself may in some way have weakened or altered the constitution of his plants, possibly by the use of raw manure or a soluble fertiliser, or even by following an unsuitable rotation. This can have the effect of making the plants more palatable or more easily accessible to the insect nuisance. In such cases it is often preferable to try to strengthen the plants by foliar sprays rather than to attack the nuisance direct. (There is one school of thought which avers that the nuisance itself has a potentiality for introducing a missing trace element and is there to restore an overall balance). It is also possible that soil conditions—compaction or excess of water—may be responsible for weakening the plant, and a timely cultivation may solve the problem.

Nettles as a Foliar Spray and a Tonic

The cheapest, easiest and quite effective foliar spray is made from stinging nettles. Fill a suitable container with nettles gathered at any stage up to flowering and add water until they are all immersed. After 24–48 hours the strained liquid diluted at about one part to four of water is effective against aphids and caterpillars; this effect may be due to the formic acid in the stinging hairs which subsequently disintegrates. If kept for a fortnight or more the strained liquid—*jauche* (German for 'liquid manure'—at the same dilution, is an excellent tonic when liberally sprayed on foliage and soil. Two refinements of this remedy are helpful. If the nettles are enclosed in a cloth or sacking bag which can be squeezed to expel the liquid, further straining is unnecessary and the rather gelatinous, partly decomposed leaves do not clog the sprayer. The other tip is to put a little of the valerian preparation 507 into the container; this will greatly reduce the unpleasant smell which accompanies the rotting of the leaves and stems. Proprietary brands of seaweed extract are alternatives to nettles. Foliar sprays of this nature are best applied during the late afternoon or evening. For crops like broad beans or brassicas with very shiny leaves, a little soft soap can be incorporated in the spray to help it to 'stick'.

If as a last resort one is forced to use an insecticide, then it is best to choose one of natural origin such as derris or pyrethrum. Nature has ways and means of dealing with these so that they do not persist in the soil and get absorbed by the crop: but no microorganisms have yet evolved to dispose of some synthetic compounds. Furthermore, up to the present no insect species has developed a means of acquiring resistance to the action of natural substances. It must, however, be borne in mind that these natural insecticides are comprehensive and will kill friend and foe alike. They must therefore be used sparingly and with discretion so that as little as possible falls on the soil to the detriment of the soil population; and if the affected crop is in flower, spraying must be done after the bees have gone to bed.

Ashes

In his course of lectures on *Agriculture* Rudolf Steiner indicated another method of combating insect nuisances. As regards reproduction, insects (and animals) are obviously closely connected with certain cosmic rhythms from which man has largely become free. If particular insects so proliferate as to become a pest, their reproductive force can largely be hindered by burning a quantity in a wood fire as described for weed seeds (pp. 81–2). Rudolf Steiner has mentioned that insects are very much influenced by the position of the sun in the zodiac. While it is passing through the constellations of the Waterman, Fishes, Ram, Bull, Twins and Crab it is radiating forces that have to do with the insect world. A favourable time for burning many insects, especially those with a chitinous exoskeleton, is when the sun and moon are both in the constellation of the Bull which will be when there is a new moon between 13 May and 20 June. The insects can be captured, killed and kept in readiness for the occasion. The quantity of ash will inevitably be very small even with all the wood ash, and a thorough dispersion may present difficulties. They may be mixed with fine sand or stirred in water as for preparation 501. One can also soak the dead insects in water for at least a month when the moon is in the Crab and spray the diluted liquid at monthly intervals under the same constellation. This method as a whole is most suitable for dealing with situations where a nuisance recurs year after year in spite of other precautionary measures. Nematodes could be a case in point.

Maria Thun has found that particular insects are affected by particular constellations. Details can be found in her booklet, *Weed and Pest Control. Based on Research into the Effects of Constellations and Potencies*.

Many claims have been made for the success of using various herbs as deterrent companion plants. Although the idea has undoubted merits from the holistic standpoint, the method cannot be relied on to be effective and there are probably other so far undiscovered factors which may affect the outcome. Mention will be made of the better attested examples under individual crops.

Wasps

These rather unattractive creatures are usually looked on with hostility by the gardener, but they are nevertheless to a certain extent our friends. In the early stages when a colony is being built up the larvae are fed largely on insects which are gathered first by the queen herself and then by the workers as they emerge: aphids are one of their sources of nourishment. It is only later, when the top fruit begins to ripen, that they become nuisances, and their habit of making small holes at the stalk ends of immature pears is particularly irritating. The time has then come to exterminate the nests (if they can be found). One need have no qualms in doing this because there will still be plenty of queens from undiscovered nests to carry on in the ensuing year, and the annoying workers are at any rate nearly at the end of their life span. Nests may be destroyed without using persistent poisons, either by squirting a pyrethrum solution into the nest after dark, or by a liberal dusting of derris round the entrance during dry weather.

Ants

Ants do not usually present a problem in the garden except that a species of black ants is often responsible for bringing and distributing blackfly on beans. One of the important functions of ants in nature's household is the regulation of formic acid in very dilute amounts in the environment which is absolutely essential for the life processes in nature. There does not seem to be any tried method of biological control; anyone who has ever tried to capture worker ants to burn for the Steiner method knows it to be an impossible task! It should not, however, be difficult to collect adults at the time of the mating flights. Otherwise it may be unavoidable in serious cases to resort to a borax/sugar poison or to a Japanese product the composition of which seems to be a trade secret.

Beetles

In this very large and varied group we have both friends and foes. Among the former are the ladybirds and most of the ground beetles which are carnivorous and act as predators on such nuisances as aphids and slugs. On the other side we have already met the wireworms, but there are also the soil-dwelling grubs of chafers, maybugs and so on. It takes them up to four years to reach full size before pupating. They are dirty white in front with swollen, rather bulbous hind parts, greyish black in colour. They feed on plant roots and on occasions can be very destructive: the adults are foliage feeders. Weevils are another branch of the beetle family; several of the more notorious will be described with the specific crops which they attack.

Spiders

Though not true insects, spiders are closely related to them and form an important link in nature's regulatory processes. They belong to a group of the Arthropods known as the Araneae; nearly all of them are carnivorous, feeding mostly on insect species which are not particularly friendly towards the gardener. They are spread out through the biosphere in every conceivable type of habitat, natural or artificial, but many people only become aware of them in human dwellings where their virtues are often the reverse of being appreciated. The species which live outside are usually unnoticed except on dewy mornings when the webs of the millions which may live on an acre of meadow or lawn glisten so beautifully in the early sunlight. There is not much a gardener can do to encourage them; but a recognition of their presence by occasionally searching for them and studying their amazing habits of life can be a stimulating experience for a gardener and perhaps in a roundabout way for the spiders themselves.

Mites

For the most part mites are very small creatures difficult to spot with the naked eye. Some species are important agents in breaking down organic matter in soil and compost; others can be a nuisance on plants if their predators are destroyed and they get out of control. There is, however, one not very commonly noticed species which is an unsuspected friend. It is the velvet mite, a brilliant scarlet creature about the size of a large mustard seed when fully grown. It lives in the surface soil and shows up mainly when seed beds are being prepared. At first one gets the impression that it may be lying in wait for juicy germinating seedlings; but in fact it is carnivorous and can be a useful predator.

Some of the newer scientific methods of controlling insects, though superficially seeming to be 'biological', may appear repulsive to sensitive people and will be dismissed on ethical grounds. For instance, use is now being made of cultures of a virus which attacks and destroys caterpillars of the cabbage white butterflies, but it is not entirely specific in its action and may destroy friends and neutrals as well. In any case, at the present stage of our knowledge of viral infection, there must always lurk the possibility of unsuspected side effects appearing after indiscriminate dispersal. Then there is the idea of trapping or confusing male insects by using artificial pheromones, the substances given off in extremely dilute amounts by females to attract their mates. If traps are baited in this way, there is always quite a strong possibility that the males will have done their job before being caught; and again, can we be quite sure that the release of these substances in greater concentrations than natural will have no unsuspected subtle effects? Another method which probably will not concern us in our temperate climate is applicable only to those species whose females, having once been covered by a male, will not copulate again: the African tsetse flies are a case in point. If, therefore, large numbers of males are bred in captivity, and then sterilised radioactively before release at the start of the breeding season, many females will lay sterile eggs. In a rather more acceptable category, some glasshouse crops are now being simultaneously inoculated with a major pest and its most effective predator, so creating a low profile balance throughout the season.

Finally, systemic insecticides are becoming popular. These are mostly synthetic substances, often based on naturally occurring compounds; they are sprayed onto plants and absorbed by the leaves, rendering them toxic to the pest in question (and presumably toxic to any humans or animals who consume them too soon after the spray has been applied). All the methods described above provide a conscientious gardener or ecologist with moral choices which are not always easy to resolve. The enormous strides made recently in gene technology may well cause alarm. Inoculating plants with another viral pathogen in order to produce immunity from a common viral disease may have devastating effects in the future, should the new virus become widely distributed via related wild species or other susceptible plants. Should one be wary of this or that variety bred to be immune from some disease?

Immunity to herbicides and certain antibiotics which are often combined is another dangerous technique which might accidentally spread to animals and humans.

Bacillus thuringiensis has long been sold commercially as a 'biological' insecticide. It forms toxins which damage fatally the intestines of caterpillars. All right for cabbage whites, but what about other harmless or even beneficial species of lepidoptera?

In this chapter an attempt has been made to depict in a rather superficial general way how the great kingdom of the insects, with all its own complicated internal relationships, is very closely connected with the plants below it and to a lesser extent with the vertebrates above it. With a background such as this perhaps we can face the problems which beset us with more satisfying feelings than those of destructive violence so prevalent around us.

CHAPTER 13

Animal Pests

by B. Saunders-Davies

We have seen that the reproductive forces in weeds can be hindered by opposing the moon's influence through the watery element by the forces of fire and burning. Insects require, in addition, influences from certain zodiacal constellations together with the sun, moon and planets. To affect animals it is necessary to use even more specialised influences from a particular planet in a particular constellation. Rudolf Steiner gives field mice as an example, but this can be applied to other rodents, mammals and also birds. Catch a few mice, take their skins (or skin and feathers in the case of birds), dry them and burn them as previously described, when Venus is in the constellation of the Scorpion. (This time varies every year so it is necessary to consult Maria Thun's planting calendar. Remember that the constellation does not coincide with the astrological 'sign'.)

The aim is to make the soil repellant to these animals since they feel the opposing negative influence countering their reproductive forces. They will avoid the area where these ashes have been scattered. It is most effective where a large area can be treated. There have been some quite spectacular results— clearing a large building of mice in one day. The effect wears off in time but can be repeated. Some farmers have reported excellent results and use the procedure regularly. In the case of a building, the ashes must be scattered on the *soil* surrounding it and not *in* the building itself.

Slugs and Snails

These creatures are a problem. Some people have had good results using their ashes persistently or letting the bodies rot in water until they are very decomposed and then sprinkling this brew several times, when the moon is in the Crab, over the worst-infected places (M. Thun). But after a mild winter and in a wet climate nothing seems to daunt them. Small areas can be protected to a certain extent by spreading sharp ashes, soot, chopped gorse, pine needles, lime (where the plants do not object to it) and using various traps such as jars sunk in the soil and baited with milk or beer. Strips of material such as cardboard, wood or slates can be laid to attract them as shelter where they can be collected.

There is a product on the market called Nemaslug which is a nematode that kills slugs, and of course the usual slug pellets.

In Switzerland an ingenious electric fence is obtainable, useful to protect small areas such as beds of seedlings. It consists of a strip of plastic about 20 to 25 cms (8 to 10 ins) wide, on which are two strands of wire, so spaced that any slug crawling up would touch the wires and get an electric shock from the small battery attached. The strip is pressed into the soil around the area to be protected. Unfortunately this device is not obtainable in Britain.

CHAPTER 14

Top Fruit

This chapter only deals with fruit trees in a small garden or in a larger one which could accommodate 20–25 trees mainly for home use. Although many of the basic principles discussed apply equally to a commercial orchard, conditions are rather different as regards labour, equipment, management and so on. For instance, a little scab on home-grown apples is not of much consequence, but a commercial grower must take extra precautions against it. Again, high yield is of prime importance commercially, but for the home more attention can be given to flavour and keeping quality.

Starting from scratch, the first step is to decide what varieties to grow in order to keep up a supply for as long a period as possible, Early maturing varieties of apple, for example, are at their best when eaten more or less straight off the tree and deteriorate rapidly if stored; others will have lost their flavour by Christmas. Plums of course cannot be stored, and pears require very special conditions of storage if they are to last for more than a month after picking. Suitability to local conditions is a major factor to consider when making a selection. A reliable nurseryman in the neighbourhood will be able to give good advice, but it might be disastrous to trust the average garden centre. Good advice can usually be obtained from members of the local garden club or horticultural society. Be particularly careful before selecting Cox's Orange Pippin because it often does not thrive from the Midlands northwards. If there is a good nursery within easy reach it is a good plan to go and choose your trees while they are still in the ground: some people recommend putting your name tag on a north (or south) facing branch so that when you come to plant it out you can orientate it in a position to which it has become accustomed. When making a selection it is also important to bear in mind that some varieties are self-sterile—that is, they cannot set any fruit from their own pollen—so it is necessary to plant occasional pollinators. James Grieve is a good apple for this purpose. This aspect loses its significance if there are plenty of trees on adjoining properties.

Types of Tree

Whatever merits may be claimed for fruit harvested from tall spreading apple or pear trees, standard and even half-standard trees are no longer popular and in any case are not really suited to a small or medium-sized garden. The tendency is to favour some type of bush tree or cordons, but fan-trained trees are very useful on south- or west-facing walls and palings. Fans are more suited to peaches, cherries, plums and pears than to apples. In small gardens especially cordons are a boon; they can be planted close together along a border or boundary and provide an opportunity to grow a wide range of varieties in a small space. There are two or three ways of training and pruning bush type trees, but this is not the place to describe them in detail. Trees can be bought as one-year-olds (maidens), or as two- or three-year-olds. In the first case the purchaser has to try to form the framework of his choice and will have to wait longer for his first fruit. Two-year-olds will have the first rudiments of a framework and in three-year-olds the main branching system will be fully developed. Espaliers are also out of favour; they are difficult to train satisfactorily and are very expensive to buy; their place has been taken by cordons.

All fruit trees are budded or grafted onto root stocks of wild or semi-wild species which are themselves propagated vegetatively. Trees grown from seed are seldom true to the parent type and take much longer to come into bearing. In recent years many refinements have been introduced into the production of root stocks and it is now possible to buy trees which will grow to the size required and no further: it was the discovery of a 'dwarfing' stock which made the cordon a possibility. A reliable nurseryman will advise you on the type of stock that is necessary for your particular needs; he will have the same variety of apple, for instance, grafted onto several different stocks—so make sure you get the right one.

Planting

Most nurserymen lift their stock in November, as soon as most of the leaves have dropped, and this is also the best time to plant out so that the new roots have a chance to develop before the next leaves come out in the spring. It is, however, best to get the holes ready before this, in July or August, to allow for a certain amount of weathering, warming and aeration to take place. The soil removed from the hole when placed in small mounds nearby will also be enlivened. With a spade take out a hole 60 cm (2 ft) square and 45 cm (18 in) deep. If the land is under grass, remove the turf with a few centimetres of soil to a radius of 90 cm (3 ft) round the planting point and stack this separately—it will come in useful for filling the bottom of the hole later on. When digging the hole put the darker-coloured topsoil in one heap, the paler subsoil in another. Square holes are better than round ones because in the latter case there is a tendency for new roots to go round and round the sides of the hole like a flower pot, instead of out into the surroundings. Later on, when applying the autumn spray of 500 to the rest of the garden, keep some for treating the holes and heaps of soil.

The trees should be planted in their holes as soon as possible after receipt from the nursery, but it can be fatal to do this if conditions are very wet or frosty. Either leave them in their packing in a sheltered place or 'heel them in' until a favourable day occurs. Before planting examine the roots carefully; remove any that are damaged, making a clean cut just behind the damaged part, and shorten any that are too long to go into the hole without bending them. The actual planting is best done with two people on the job, one holding the tree in position, the other filling the hole. First put a thin pole over the centre of the hole to indicate the ground level. It is important to plant the tree at the same depth as in the nursery; shallow planting will leave some of the roots exposed, while deep planting is liable to cover the grafting union, leading to undesirable root formation from the scion and to the danger of rots entering. Loosely tie the upper roots to the trunk above so that they do not get dragged down in the early stages of filling, and put the tree in position. Fill only with topsoil and turf to which some compost should be added at intervals; there is no need to overdo the compost—half a bucketful per hole is enough if the soil is in good heart. On poorer or newly reclaimed land the amount of compost should be increased and two or three handfuls of bonemeal or hoof and horn may be added. Gently firm the soil over the roots as the work proceeds and make sure there are no air gaps left round the tap root. Release the upper roots at the appropriate time. There will not be enough topsoil to fill the hole completely; make up the deficiency from an outside source or by drawing some in from the surroundings, replacing it by spreading the heaped subsoil. Finally, tie the trunk to a stout stake to prevent windrock and apply a mulch over the surface. Make the tie in figure-of-eight form, one loop round the stake and the other round the trunk; an old nylon stocking is very good for the purpose as it is strong and will not chafe the bark. There are, however, advantages if the stake is driven into position first and the tree then planted against it: in this case special care must be taken to see that the soil is packed firmly between stake and tree and that no air pockets are left there.

After-Care

If a row of cordons or a few isolated trees have been planted along a border or close to areas under regular cultivation, there is not much to worry about except to give them an annual mulch in early summer, perhaps with a little compost, and to keep them clear of weeds. Instead of a mulch white clover to supply a little nitrogen can be established as a permanent cover, either from seed or more easily from runners. When a small orchard is being established on open ground, it is possible (perhaps even desirable) to intercrop with vegetables such as potatoes, brassicas and broad beans for a couple of years before planting a permanent sward. The compost and the use of the 500 and 501 sprays given to the vegetables will help the young trees also, but the areas immediately round the trees should be mulched annually. On the other hand a succession of green manure cover crops may be grown, alternating legumes with mustard, rape and rye. Some of the top growth from these will supply material for mulching, the rest being worked in before sowing the next cover. By either of these methods a truly fertile and living soil is made ready to take a permanent sward in the third year. The latter will consist of a mixture of grasses and clovers sown in late summer or early autumn; its exact composition of species will vary according to local conditions.

If planting has been done on meadow land, it is advisable to keep the cleared rings cultivated for a year or two with mulches and some compost. The mulch will be supplied by cutting the grass and this should be done two or three times a year, just before the grasses come into flower. Young grass and other herbage is much richer in nitrogen than any which has flowered. Spray the whole area with 500 in spring and autumn, and with 501 at least once in early summer when the young tree branchlets are in full growth. In all cases, after planting new fruit trees make a firm resolve not to allow any fruit to develop in the first year; pinch out all fruit buds as soon as they appear. It is also wise to limit fruiting in the second year.

Pruning

For detailed descriptions of the various methods of pruning the reader, if inexperienced, is advised to consult one of the excellent books or manuals noted in Appendix C. A few general remarks, however, may not be out of place here. Most fruit trees if left to themselves will develop far too many long and spindly growths, with the result that there will eventually be a lot of poor quality undersized fruit because they have been starved of air and light. The aim is to obtain a compact shape with evenly spaced branches carrying plenty of fruiting spurs. For summer pruning especially it is best to choose a period of waning moon for the work, a time when the plant sap is not rising so strongly. This is not so important for the main pruning carried out during late autumn, when the trees have lost their leaves and have gone into a dormant period. Whenever wood that is more than two years old is cut out, the wounds must be treated against the possible entry of fungi; although commercial products are satisfactory for this purpose, the fruit tree paste (see below) is better because it stimulates the cambium to cover the wound more quickly. Another point not usually mentioned in the text books is the following. When a young growth is shortened back to an outer bud, it often happens that the next bud below it develops into an unwanted side growth. The remedy is to nick out this bud with the point of a secateur blade or thumbnail, thus diverting energy into the wanted fruit buds lower down.

Tree Paste

Rudolf Steiner likens the trunk of a tree to an elongated mound of soil, hollowed out in the centre. It is not therefore altogether surprising that something akin to a soil treatment is recommended for the trunks and main branches of fruit trees. This consists of applying a paste made up to the following formula:

1 part dried blood
2 parts kieselguhr (diatomite, a form of organic silica)
3 parts clay
4 parts cowdung

It is not necessary to adhere strictly to these proportions; they are a rough guide and in fact the dried blood, though desirable, is not absolutely essential. If kieselguhr is quite unobtainable, very fine sand may be substituted. Any kind of pottery clay can be used; alternatively one may be able to get it from garden subsoil, from a new roadside cutting or perhaps from a local brickworks, depending on circumstances. As the clay has to be kneaded and worked into a slurry, a lot of hard work is saved if it can be found in an already finely divided state. The clay has a threefold purpose: it acts as a sticking agent for the paste, it seals up small crevices in which insect nuisances may be lurking, and it is a mediator between the cosmic and earthly forces. The slurry is made either with rain water, stirred 500, dilute equisetum tea or very dilute liquid manure. A mixture of the last two has much to recommend it. Having prepared the clay slurry, the dung is then worked in with the other ingredients. The dung should not be very fresh, so it will have to be obtained from a manure heap or by collecting pats two to four weeks old from a meadow where cattle have been grazing. A final refinement is to add pinches of the compost preparations 502–6 with a few drops of 507. More liquid may have to be added to bring the consistency to that of porridge made with fine oatmeal. Before putting the paste onto the trees, work over them with a wire brush to remove any loose bark, lichens or moss which may be present. Put on old clothes as some splashing is inevitable, especially if dealing with old standard trees. Apply the paste liberally with a whitewash brush, working quickly from the top without any attempt at artistic effects. The work is best done in late autumn, but any time in non-frosty weather up to the end of March is satisfactory.

Treatment of Mature Trees

Once trees in an established sward have come into bearing there is very little to be done in the way of soil treatments. The trunks should be kept clear of vegetation to a radius of 23–30 cm (9–12 in). The sward can be kept close cut with a rotary mower, in which case the cut grass is left where it lies to rot down and provide worm food. If allowed to grow longer it will have to be cut with a scythe and the hay is either used as a mulch or removed for composting with other material for eventual return to the orchard. The mulch may be applied in circles round the trees just below the ends of the outer branches where most of the feeding roots are working. Another method is to rake the grass into straight rows in the root feeding area; the second cut can then be placed in rows at right angles to the first. An occasional dressing of compost to the whole area is beneficial, but do not waste it around the bases of the trunks because the active roots there will mostly have died out. Spring and autumn sprays of 500 to the whole area are advisable. Ideally 501 is sprayed three times—first, when the tree has made its first leaves and flower buds are showing, second, when the fruitlets are the size of hazelnuts, and third, when the fruit is beginning to ripen. This is rather a daunting programme for most gardeners unless the times coincide with spraying other crops. The most important spray is the second, but if August is dull and cold the third becomes almost essential if good quality fruit is to be harvested.

Another job when a tree has set a heavy crop is to thin out the fruitlets when about the size of a walnut, but this does not apply to plums and cherries. It has been shown by experiment that one apple to 20 leaves gives the best results; there is no need to count every leaf on the tree, just do it on one or two branchlets to get the right feeling.

Insect Nuisances

When thinning apples, some fruitlets will almost certainly be found to have small holes on the sides with a little brown mess around them. Remove all of these and put them aside separately for burning because they contain a sawfly larva. Removal at this stage prevents a second generation from developing and will save quite a lot of fruit from being spoilt later on. If left alone the attacked fruits will eventually drop off and allow the mature larvae to pupate in the soil. Dropped fruit should also be collected, but it does not take the larva long to emerge when it has reached its goal, so constant attention is necessary. Another rather similar apple and pear nuisance is the codlin moth larva which enters the developing fruit later in the year (midsummer onwards) usually through the eye. It reveals it presence by frass which may be difficult to spot amongst the old sepals, and occasional inspections are advisable. The mature larvae of this species come down the main trunk looking for a secluded place to pupate and hibernate. They can be tempted by tying a roll of corrugated paper 15 cm (6 in) wide three times round the trunk about 60 cm (2 ft) from the ground. The paper is taken off in October and burned. One further apple nuisance is the wintermoth. The females are wingless and so must crawl up the trunk of a tree to lay their eggs on flower buds and young leaves. They can be trapped by putting grease bands on the trunks and any stakes when the codlin moth traps are removed. In both these cases make sure that there are no tall weed stems which can be used as ladders to and from the lower branches. A last but rarer nuisance is the woolly aphis which appears as blobs like cotton-wool on fruit tree trunks. The blobs can be destroyed by applying methylated spirit with a paint brush, and further attacks may be prevented by sowing nasturtiums under the tree.

Diseases

The chief worry for apple growers is scab which appears as small round dark patches on the fruit (and leaves); some varieties are more susceptible than others, Newton Wonder being one of the worst offenders. For a commercial grower such blemished fruit become worthless and he has to undertake a complicated pre-ventative spraying programme which can in fact be achieved by bio-dynamic methods. The home grower, however, need not be unduly troubled because the spots are only skin deep and do not affect the flavour or, more than to a minor degree, the keeping quality. Nevertheless, some precautionary steps are advisable and here again silica in one form or another comes to our aid. A prior necessity is to ensure by good pruning that plenty of light reaches all parts of the tree and that air can circulate freely. The normal sprays of 501 will provide some help. Supplementary treatments include equisetum tea (preparation 508) sprayed on trees and ground soon after fruit has set, perhaps repeated a fortnight later, and a spray of waterglass (sodium silicate) about the beginning of August at the rate of 1 oz. per gallon (10 g per litre). The same solution of waterglass can also be usefully applied to the soil (as described for gooseberries, p. 118) when growth starts in the spring and again in July. These treatments will also help against possible attacks by rust and mildew. It must again be emphasised that the major factor in disease control is a healthy, vigorous microlife in the soil.

With plums, and to a lesser extent other stone fruit, one must always be on the look-out for silver leaf disease which can be a killer. The symptoms are unmistakable: the leaves on some twigs and branches take on a silvery sheen and then sooner or later die. Immediate action is necessary if the tree is to be saved. After cutting out the affected parts, examine the cut carefully and if there is the slightest sign of brown discolouration in the wood, cut back farther until all trace of this has disappeared.

Paint the cut with a preservative and burn all the diseased parts at once. The danger of attack by silver leaf is greatly reduced by pruning all stone fruit trees in the summer rather than later in the year. More recently it has been discovered that quite a common micro-organism called *Trichoderma viride* can parasitise the silverleaf fungus and eliminate it provided that the infection is caught at an early stage. The *Trichoderma* has to be treated in such a way that it can be taken up by the sap of the tree, and it is marketed by a Swedish company as SB Binab T.

Peach leaf curl is a very common trouble on the young leaves of peaches, nectarines, cherries and almonds. They are invaded by a fungus which causes them to turn crimson and curl up. It is difficult to eradicate completely even by using the latest types of fungicide. Some gardeners have claimed good results after planting garlic round the trees, but this is not a fully reliable treatment. As with most fungus diseases, the seat of the trouble is likely to lie in the soil; so if the disease has been present in the previous year, the first thing to do is to give a loosening cultivation early in the spring when the buds are just beginning to swell. This is followed by regular spraying with equisetum tea (508) every 10–14 days combined with two applications of the waterglass soil treatment as described for gooseberries in the next chapter.

Fruit-Eating Nuisances

Blackbirds and thrushes must be suffered gladly for their joyful singing and other benefits which they bestow, but they can be restrained from undue avarice in various ways. Sometimes they may merely be thirsty, so see that there is always a bird bath handy for them, especially during dry weather. Early apples always tempt them, but their annoying habit of taking a few pecks from a lot of fruit can be counterd to a certain extent by picking the first damaged fruit and leaving them on the ground; the birds will usually prefer these to sound ones still on the tree. Cherries are very vulnerable, but some branches can be saved by pulling an old nylon stocking over them; if grown fan-trained against a wall they are easily netted. Old nylon stockings, cut into two pieces, are also very effective in thwarting wasps with their aggravating habit of making a small hole just below the stalks of unripe pears: on cordon pears in particular half a stocking can be tied to cover at least one and often two or three fruit. Squirrels are quite impossible to deal with; they rip the stockings off cherry branches and they use a low strawberry net like a trampoline, bouncing it up and down until they can reach the fruit.

CHAPTER 15

Soft Fruit

Sufficient soft fruit for a small family, including jam and bottling, can be obtained from an area of 5 m by 7 m (15 ft by 20 ft). This would take a row of raspberries, three blackcurrants, three gooseberries and two or three red or white currants. Although an area of such a size is about the minimum for giving a complete range, it does allow for planting different varieties of each type to provide a succession for harvesting over a longer period. It should even be possible to fit in a blackberry and a loganberry or tayberry, which is more vigorous, on a framework along the side. Space permitting, any of these items can of course be increased to suit individual needs. Suggested varieties are given in Appendix B.

Land for planting soft fruit is prepared in the same way as for top fruit except that growing bushes in a green sward is not recommended. It will get the bushes off to a good start if a bulky green manure crop can be grown during the summer and then worked in during September before planting out in November. Holes are taken out in the same way as described for top fruit, but the operation may have to be delayed until after a green manure crop has had time to decompose. Raspberries will require a trench rather than holes. Do not put a lot of decomposing green material into the bottom of a hole or trench; it cannot develop into the right kind of humus at such a depth. Half a bucket of compost per hole is desirable, but it need not be fully rotted down; a double handful of bonemeal mixed with hoof and horn per hole is beneficial, and any available wood ash can be spread over the whole plot. It is perhaps worth mentioning here that some growers recommend planting bush fruit on raised beds or ridges: I have only slight experience of this practice, but on very heavy land it would be well worth trying. In this case a gently sloping ridge 120–150 cm (4–5 ft) wide will have to be constructed, giving a 23–30 cm (9–12 in) drop between crest and trough.

Mulching is undoubtedly the best after-treatment for all soft fruit throughout their lives: it solves the weed problem provided that all perennial weeds have been scrupulously removed during land preparation, and it provides a regular supply of worm food. Straw, if obtainable, is very good for this purpose, and can be supplemented with autumn leaves or half-rotted leaf mould from the previous year. It is best applied in the autumn so as to retain some of the summer warmth. Before putting on any mulch the remains of the last one are scratched into the top few centimetres of the soil and any compacted patches are loosened with a fork, always remembering that the fine feeding roots of all soft fruit are very close to the surface. Then spread a little compost, together with all the wood ashes and bonfire ash that can be collected. Finally, again before the mulch, spray with 500; if no bio-dynamic compost has been put on, pinches of the compost preparations should be added to the 500 before stirring. Another possibility is to mulch with deep litter from a poultry house. This *must* be applied in the late autumn when the roots are dormant, otherwise some raw nitrogenous substances may be taken up which will lead to overlush growth susceptible to diseases. If material for mulching is quite unobtainable, the plants will require more compost than would be used under a mulch; when put on in the spring it should be well ripened, but an autumn application should be less mature.

All soft fruits need plenty of potash. If the compost has been made with a good proportion of poultry or pig manure, the potash supply should be adequate; but cow manure or the average type of compost will have be supplemented. Wood ashes provide the best answer, but they *must* be kept dry: if left out in the rain after a fire, much of their potash will be lost by leaching. In a larger garden a patch of Russian comfrey can be grown and its potash-rich leaves can be used as a mulch. Even so it is unlikely that there will be enough to treat the whole plot every year and a system of rotational applications will have to be worked out. A foliar spray of comfrey *jauche* soon after fruitset can also help.

501 is sprayed ideally three times—when the flower buds are just beginning to appear, soon after the fruit has set and after harvest when the leaves are nourishing next year's buds. The second of these is the most important.

Raspberries

The normal life of a raspberry cane is three years. In the first year a small shoot is formed at the base of an earlier cane or from a point on a larger root, but it does not appear above the soil. In the second year the shoots develop into fully grown canes but do not flower. In the third year flower-bearing shoots grow out from the buds formed at the bases of the previous year's leaves. After bearing their crop these canes die and are replaced by the next generation. There are, however, varieties that fruit in the autumn on current season canes brought into growth by cutting back all except very young shoots in March; much of such fruit often fails to ripen properly. It is best to start a raspberry bed with bought-in plants which are certified as virus-free. Even if they have been maltreated with chemicals they will soon lose any hankering after them and will respond to bio-dynamic treatments. The bought plants will consist of a cane up to 60 cm (2 ft) long and should have at least one shoot 5–7.5 cm (2–3 in) long at the base where the roots come out. They are planted 38 cm (15 in) apart, so a dozen plants will occupy 5 m (15 ft) of row. If planting a double row do not be led astray by the usual text book advice to space the rows 150 cm (5 ft) apart; give them an extra 30 cm—it will make picking and other operations much more convenient. Planting is best done in the autumn but may be deferred until early spring. Take out a trench 45 cm (18 in) wide and 30 cm (12 in) deep and as usual keeping the top and subsoil separate. On a heavy soil fork over the bottom of the trench to break it up a little and help drainage. About six buckets of nearly rotted compost or well rotted manure will be needed for the 5 m (15 ft) trench, but it must not be put in below

15 cm (6 in). One kilo (2 lb) each of bonemeal and hoof and horn are also advisable. The trench is filled as for top fruit holes. The young plants must not be set too deep down in the trench; a good guide is to put them in so that not much more than 25 mm (1 in) of soil will cover the small young shoots.

The usual practice is then to fix training wires for the canes to prevent wind damage and to support the crop. Old telephone wire, if obtainable, is very good for this purpose. A stout post with its last 60 cm (2 ft) well creosoted is planted firmly at each end of the row and wires are stretched between them at 90, 120 and 150 cm (3, 4 and 5 ft) above ground level. An intermediate less stout post will prove to be a good addition as 5 m (15 ft) is rather on the long side for keeping the wires reasonably taut. An alternative method is to dispense with wires altogether after the first two years. In this way a kind of hedge is developed, allowing more canes to grow out from each stool than is possible under a strict training programme. There will be a certain amount of mutual support without excessive overcrowding, but the outer canes will tend to droop when carrying a heavy crop.

After planting, the canes on the new plants are cut back to four buds: the leaves from these will help to nourish the sprouting shoots in their early stages, but any feeble attempts by these older buds to flower and fruit must be frustrated. In the second and future years the old canes are cut out as soon as harvesting is complete. At the same time young weaklings and any canes surplus to future requirements are removed, leaving four per stool. The temptation to leave more than four must be resisted because overcrowding on the wires is one of the main causes of mouldy fruit in damp weather. At this stage the new canes are loosely slid between the wires. When the buds begin to swell in the spring (February/March) tip back all the canes to a strong bud and fix them with two ties to the appropriate wires, leaving no growth much above the 150 cm (5 ft) wire. Buds at the tips, if not pruned back, do not bear the best fruit, so it is better to concentrate the plant sap into stronger growths. This job should not be done before bud swelling as there is a danger of frost damage and die-back.

There are several troubles to prevent or watch for. As mentioned above, raspberries may get infected by virus, the commonest being indicated by a bronzing and mottling of the leaves with a consequent deterioration in the size and quality of the fruit. These symptoms are unlikely to appear in a well established bio-dynamic garden, but the virus could be present or dormant in old stools on a recently acquired property. Early diagnosis is made difficult by the fact that the very young leaves of some varieties tend to have a bronze tinge. There is no proved cure for this trouble, either conventional or bio-dynamic. An infected row will have to be eradicated and another one started on a new site well away from the old one.

The raspberry beetle *Byturus tomentosus* can become a nuisance. It is a small pale brown creature which lays its eggs in the flowers, and the emerging larvae ('maggots') eat their way into the fruit. The standard remedy is to spray the flowering shoots with derris two or three times during the season, but this can be very dangerous for bees unless the treatment is done in the evening when they have ceased working. This rather drastic remedy should never be used unless there has been serious damage in the previous year and unless the beetles have actually been seen. In any case, collect and burn any damaged fruit. The larvae pupate in the soil round the stools where they pass the winter, so it may be a good plan to work over the soil very gently two or three times during autumn and winter in the hope that robins will find the pupae.

In damp, dull weather the fruit may go mouldy due to attack by botrytis. If such conditions prevail when the fruit is setting, a preventative spray of equisetum (508) repeated at seven to ten day intervals will be a help, though it may not be 100 per cent effective. Other preventative measures will include the normal spray of 501, the avoidance of a spring application of any raw manure, and perhaps the waterglass treatment described below for gooseberries.

Gooseberries

Gooseberries are most conveniently grown on a 'leg'—that is, with about 15 cm (6 in) of clear stem before any branches are allowed to grow. If purchased from a nursery two-year-old plants are to be preferred because the basic framework will have been formed by the nurseryman, and they will be easier than three-year-olds to establish under bio-dynamic conditions. It is not difficult, however, to strike cuttings from one's own bushes or from a friend's: the main point here is to cut out cleanly *all* buds below those which will eventually form the framework: any bits of buds on the part of the cutting below ground level will shoot all too easily and create a multi-stemmed bush very quickly.

Planting is done in the usual way during autumn in holes spaced 150 cm (5 ft) apart. A slightly raised bed may help to ward off mildew. After planting shorten the leading branches by about one third to an upward and outward facing bud. Subsequent pruning will consist of shortening the leaders and reducing side growths to two buds to form fruit spurs, the latter operation being done in July. After some years the leaders and spurs on the main branches may start to lose vigour: they can be cut out to a strong new shoot which will probably have been formed near the centre of the bush. Long-established bushes with a mass of shoots arising from the base should be drastically thinned, cutting out the oldest and weakest and leaving only a few strong growths. When pruning gooseberries the main point is to make picking as easy and painless as possible, so try to imagine what the bush will look like when carrying a heavy crop.

There are two common troubles. First is the sawfly (*Nematus ribesii*) whose larvae can defoliate a bush very quickly if given full rein. They are green and spotty, almost translucent, and their presence is soon betrayed by the little black specks of their excrement on the leaves below. They usually start on the young shoots on the lower centre part of the bush from mid-April onwards. Derris dust will deal with them, or they can be hand picked if caught at the earliest stage of their activity: if this batch is not tackled at once, a second more numerous generation will emerge three weeks later. The second trouble is mildew which starts as white spots on the developing fruit and soon covers them with a sort of grey felt which later spreads to the young shoots. This is a case where prevention is better than cure, for even regular spraying with 508 is not very effective once the mildew has become established. The first precaution is to ensure that the soil around the bushes is not compacted and that no raw or half rotted manure is used. Lime sulphur at the recommended dose sprayed when growth is starting and again a month later is said to give good protection, but some varieties are 'sulphur shy' and the young leaves will be killed. Waterglass (sodium silicate) at a strength of 25 g (1 oz) per 4.5 litres (1 gal) seems to help but has not been proved over a long period: it is sprayed as for 508. At the same time a little of the solution at double strength is poured into small holes half a trowel deep and spaced 90 cm (3 ft) apart under the extremities of the outer branches. Slightly attacked fruit can be washed and cooked. Strangely enough mildew can be even more devastating in very dry weather than when it is wet.

Blackcurrants

Blackcurrants are planted in the same way as gooseberries. The planting distance may be as little as 120 cm (4 ft), but unless space saving is of prime importance 150 cm (5 ft) allows for greater ease of picking, weeding and cultivation. They are propagated by 20–25 cm (8–10 in) cuttings taken in autumn from young growth which has just shed its leaves, making sure that any rounded buds are taken off and burned. The lower buds are not removed as for gooseberries because plenty of growth from the base is desirable: they will have to remain in the bed for two years before planting out, and it will then be another year before a small crop can be expected. Bought-in plants will probably have three or four shoots on them: these are cut back to about four buds which will produce the fruiting stems for the following year.

Most of the crop is borne on the young pale-coloured growths of the previous year. Any older black-coloured branches and stems will make some shoots during the growing season, but these are usually short and thin, and will not carry the best fruit. The object of management and pruning is to stimulate long, strong shoots at or near the base of the bush. This is achieved by pruning out all branches which have borne a crop right back to the base or to a strong shoot not less than 45 cm (18 in) long. Pruning is done as soon as the last currant has been picked, thus concentrating all the plant's energy into next year's crop. Mature bushes which have been allowed to retain a lot of old wood are best treated over two years, cutting half the old branches right back to leave only 7.5–10 cm (3–4 in) of stump from which strong shoots will spring in the following year.

The demand on the plant for vigorous growth every year means that it will need more nitrogen than other soft fruit. This is given by compost or manure at up to two buckets per bush, applied in the autumn. First loosen any compacted patches with a fork and spray with preparation 500. Then, after spreading the manure, cover with a straw mulch. If the work has to be deferred till the spring, only fully ripened compost should be used. An alternative to the autumn compost/straw combination is deep litter from a poultry house, when available: it is spread 5 cm (2 in) deep around the bushes.

Apart from greenfly, the chief trouble with blackcurrants is likely to come from 'big bud'. It is caused by tiny mites which enter the buds while they are still growing and cause them to develop into a larger spherical form instead of the normal smaller and more tapering shape. As soon as the buds begin to swell in the spring, the mites feed on the embryo flower stalks within and then migrate to other buds. The standard remedy is lime sulphur applied when the leaves are just opening and again later, but as with gooseberries some varieties do not like this treatment. With only a few bushes hand picking is quite possible at any time during late autumn or winter, but it is essential to go over the bushes two or three times because it is almost impossible to spot all the infected buds at the first picking. Burn the buds in an open tin over a hot wood fire, mix the white ash with fine sand and scatter it round the bushes, or else treat the ash like 501. This will not provide an immediate cure, but will help if repeated over three or four years.

The 'big bud' mite is liable to carry the virus which causes a condition known as 'reversion': in other words the bushes revert to a wild state, bearing undersized fruit and small leaves with only three points instead of the usual five or more. There is no known remedy: infected bushes must be uprooted and burned and a fresh start made in a different part of the garden. When moving into an old garden it is advisable to inspect any old blackcurrant bushes very carefully for signs of this disease before deciding whether to keep them.

Red and White Currants

The treatment of both types is the same, so they are taken together: in fact it almost seems that originally one of them sprang from the other. Here again 150 cm (5 ft) spacing is to be preferred to 120 cm (4 ft). The fruit is borne on both old and young wood, so training and pruning are quite different from blackcurrants, in fact much the same as for gooseberries. Both are best grown on a 'leg' with four well-spaced main branches from which strong outward-growing laterals are allowed to develop so as to fill out the bush without overcrowding it. Smaller and inward-growing laterals are cut back to three buds soon after harvest in order to promote the formation of fruit buds for the following year. If multi-stemmed plants are bought or inherited, they should be treated as if the 'leg' had been buried and was forking at ground level. Only four or at most five main stems are needed, and all young shoots springing from the base are cut right back during autumn pruning when leaders and main laterals are shortened by a third. These currants are liable to get rather straggly with age, but this habit can be corrected by cutting the main branches back to a strong growth near the centre. Soil treatment and the use of 500 and 501 follow the same lines as for gooseberries.

The only fairly common trouble is due to aphis attack quite early in the season. The growing leaves develop small red patches which enlarge with the leaf, turning a dark crimson and distorting the normal shape. By the time the bulbous-looking blotches become obvious it is too late to do anything about them, but the damage is not very serious. It is not difficult to spot the trouble in its early stages, and a spray or dusting with derris, pyrethrum or nettle *jauche* should clear things up.

These currants, and gooseberries also, can be planted against a wall or fence and trained either as cordons at 30 cm (1 ft) apart or as fans at 75 cm (2 ft 6 in). This method is very convenient for netting and makes picking easier. An annual mulch of compost, manure or deep litter is given in the autumn with 500: this helps to retain moisture, but in a dry summer some irrigation may be necessary.

Blackberries, Loganberries and Tayberries

It is well worth growing at least one plant of each if the necessary space can be found. Each will require a 300 cm (10 ft) run of three or four training wires stretched between supporting posts. Propagation is simple. In September the tip of a young cane is pegged down to the soil and covered with a piece of slate or tile. By the end of November it will have developed a mass of roots and a small young shoot. The cane is cut at 60 cm (2 ft) from the young plant which is lifted and transferred to a well composted nursery bed for a year before being moved to its permanent position. At this stage the old piece of cane will have died, and there should be a strong shoot about 90 cm (3 ft) long with an embryo shoot at its base, just like a raspberry. This is what one gets if purchasing from a nursery. Planting is done in the usual way and the leading cane is taken back to about half a dozen buds. The new cane should attain several feet and will bear fruit in the following year. Cultural treatment in subsequent years is similar to that for other soft fruit.

Again like raspberries, the canes die after bearing a crop and must be cut back to the ground soon after harvest is over; but on some very vigorous blackberries only the ends and the side fruit-bearing branchlets die off and it is possible to keep the main cane for cropping in the second year. After three years or so quite large stools will have developed and they will produce a lot of young canes every season. With loganberries and tayberries, a way has to be found to prevent them interfering with the ripening crop. There are four possibilities:

1 Leave them alone and put up with the inconvenience: at least the young growth will give some protection from birds.

2 Train all bearing canes to one side of the stool and the young ones to the other, reversing in the following year, but this method does not make full use of the available space.

3 Bundle the young canes round a tall central pole as they grow—not at all easy.

4 Gently bend each young cane over to the left or right as appropriate when it has reached a length of about 120 cm (4 ft) and tie in bundles very loosely to the lowest training wire.

Methods 1 and 4 are the most practical.

After cutting out the old canes the young ones are spread loosely over the training wires where they will continue to grow. The final training is left until the leaves have dropped off in February or March. One, or at the most two, of the strongest canes are twined round each of the top three wires, giving a maximum of twelve canes per stool. Damaged and weak canes surplus to requirements are cut out at ground level, only one bud is left on any side shoots which may have arisen, and the ends of the trained canes are taken back to a strong bud near the supporting posts.

Blackberries are easier to deal with as they do not produce so many young canes from the base, and it is not so necessary to sort these out from those bearing the crop: four strong canes per stool will give a good crop because each flowering side branch carries much more fruit than on a loganberry or tayberry. Pruning and training are similar to loganberries and tayberries. Although varieties are mentioned in Appendix B, it is perhaps appropriate here to give a word of warning about Himalayan Giant. Its large fruit are of reasonable quality, but its thorns are particularly vicious and it produces canes of six metres (20 ft) or more which are very difficult to manage.

These fruits are susceptible to the raspberry beetle, and the same methods of dealing with it are applicable. In a wet year logans may suffer from botrytis mould which will be more damaging in crowded conditions—an argument against method 1 above. Again treat as for raspberries. Logans may also develop 'smutty nose', a trouble not mentioned in any text book. As the name implies, the pips at the ends of the fruit do not swell and generally become dark in colour. It is probably a physiological trouble brought on partly by the greed of the grower in leaving too many canes to fruit, and partly by a shortage of potash. The remedy is obvious.

Tayberries are the result of a cross similar to loganberries but are more vigorous and tolerant. The flavour is excellent. When very ripe, almost purple, they can be eaten as dessert but are particularly good for stewing, bottling or freezing. It is worth planting a few along a stretch of posts and wires if you can afford the space. Propagation is by pegging the tip of a young cane into the ground or a pot.

Strawberries

Strawberries fall into a category of their own, quite different from bush fruit. Their maximum useful life is only three years, or four under exceptionally good conditions. It is not advisable to replant in the same place after uprooting the worn-out plants, so some form of rotation is called for. Strawberries cannot conveniently be fitted into the vegetable rotation unless large quantities are needed and there is plenty of space: in such a case an extra plot would have to be incorporated and they would occupy one plot for four years, following root crops and followed by brassicas. A better arrangement is to devote part of the garden to strawberries and to divide it into three plots. One plot would carry them for two years, the other two being used for fertility building and odd vegetables such as sweet corn which do not fit easily into the main plan: salad crops could also be grown here. In the first year take runners (as described below) from any existing strong plants, or buy them in, certified virus-free, from a reliable source. Plant them out as soon as possible in late July or early August. Leave these to fruit a second year, and take runners from them then for the next planting. The plot which is to take them will have been sown the previous autumn with winter tares and rye to give a good bulk for digging in during the latter half of May. The green manure will be well decomposed for the runners in July, and could stand an intercrop of lettuce. It would be quite possible under this system to leave the original bed for a third year and postpone the planting of the next one, but the largest and finest berries are borne on maidens and two-year-old plants.

Although new strawberries may be planted at any time during late summer, autumn or even in the spring (in which case they must be disbudded), by far the best results are obtained from runners established in late July or early August. In order to get them ready in time the first ones from the strongest bearing plants are either pegged into the soil where they will not interfere with picking, or are pegged into 7.5 cm (3 in). pots filled with a rich compost mixture and sunk into the bed. In either case any growth beyond the pegged runner is regularly removed. In very dry weather the pots may need a little water from time to time. The object is to produce as early as possible vigorous runners which will continue to develop strongly well into the autumn after being planted out. Runners planted out in September or October (as is often done) do not get a chance to make a root system capable of nourishing more than a couple of bearing trusses in the following season. When planting out great care must be taken to spread the roots well and not too deeply, and to ensure that that the crown is firmly in position level with the soil surface.

Strawberries prefer a slightly acid soil, and for this reason pine needles are often recommended as a mulch to be applied in April or May before the first blossoms open. Pine needles are less attractive to slugs than the usual straw mulch, and their aroma improves the quality of the fruit. For plants which are to be retained a generous dressing of compost with a sprinkling of bonemeal or very well rotted manure is lightly worked into the soil with the remains of the mulch soon after harvest, but first remove all surplus runners and give a spray of 500. In this way the plants are enabled to build up good crowns for the following year: but on light soils liable to winter leaching the dressing is best deferred until the spring.

Apart from birds the main troubles are greenfly and botrytis mould. The greenfly start right in the hearts among the youngest leaves and are not always obvious to casual inspection: rather than hope for predators to arrive, it is better to deal with them at once with nettle *jauche* or derris squirted well into the crowns. Botrytis attack can be severe in dull, damp seasons. The normal 501 sprays at bud formation and first ripening will afford some protection, but it is best to supplement these with regular equisetum treatment at weekly intervals from fruit set if conditions appear to be adverse. In gardens where the trouble has appeared in the past irrespective of the weather, it is worth trying the waterglass treatment. In any event do not tempt the botrytis by leaving dead leaves and old fruit stalks on older plants: remove them in March, or April at the latest.

Strawberries should be planted and cultivated preferably on fruit days. In damp climates especially, and to discourage fungal attack, it is a good idea to plant them on slightly raised beds— two rows to a bed. It raises them a little above the 'fungi level' of the soil and they are also easier to pick.

Birds

For soft fruit the question whether to net or not is a difficult one. On a commercial scale netting is not only impossible but is also quite unnecessary; in a small garden the percentage of fruit taken is likely to be very much larger. The one or two redcurrant bushes which are quite sufficient for the needs of a family must be netted, otherwise thrushes will strip the lot before they are fully ripe. Blackcurrants are not so tempting and a good crop can usually be obtained from unprotected bushes. Raspberries and logans are borderline; sometimes it seems that birds regard nets as a challenge to their ingenuity. If there are bullfinches around it may be necessary to protect gooseberries from their ravages between Christmas and Easter; it does not take a pair of them very long to take all the buds off a bush, leaving only those at the ends of the twigs. Apart from almost total loss of crop the bare twigs are useless for further bearing, and the bush will have to be pruned down to a skeleton. A small patch of strawberries is extremely vulnerable and must be netted unless the plants are under cloches.

One solution to the problem is to have a fruit cage. The old-fashioned type, small mesh wire netting stapled to a stout timber framework, is now prohibitively expensive to erect and maintain; but synthetic fibre netting on a frame of interlocking aluminium rods is well worth consideration. It must, however, be remembered that it is essential to remove at least the top net during the offseason, both to allow access to birds looking for insects and to avoid heavy accumulations of snow which may bend the frame, rupture the net and break the fruit bushes.

CHAPTER 16

Vegetable Crops

For ease of reference the commonest vegetable crops, together with some not so common, have been grouped under seven headings according to the part of the plant which serves as food; they are in alphabetical order under each heading. Detailed cultural instructions, which can be found in any good text book, are not included; but attention has been focused on special features derived from personal experience, on preventing or dealing with troubles, and on particular bio-dynamic practices. Recommended varieties are given in Appendix B.

BRASSICAS

The Brassica family in one form or another is welcomed in the kitchen throughout the year. They are all very greedy feeders, and on light, sandy soil it is sometimes a problem to supply their full needs.

For early spring use one relies chiefly on the various sprouting broccoli, sown in May/June and transplanted in late summer. A good succession is provided in this order by white sprouting, purple sprouting, Pentland Brig and asparagus kale (if one can find the seed); this succession should last from mid-March until the end of May. Pentland Brig is a vigorous, branching, good-flavoured curly kale whose young leaves can be used from January onwards; if the plants are given a rest when the white sprouting starts, they will produce a mass of very palatable flowering shoots in late April/early May. The plants must be spaced at least 90 cm (3 ft) apart, but unfortunately they do not tolerate very severe frosts though they will come through an average winter. The various headed broccoli come to fruition during this period, but it is doubtful if they are worth growing in a small garden because they occupy a disproportionate amount of space over a long period just to provide one meal.

For summer use, apart from spring cabbage which has lain dormant in situ through the winter, there are the quick growing cabbages and cauliflowers. They can be sown in boxes under cover in February/March, pricked out at 5–7.5 cm (2–3 in) apart in a frame at the two-leaf stage, and finally transplanted in May for use in July/August. If space permits some of the seedlings may be left in the frame to come on earlier. The chief difficulty here is late frost which gives the plants a severe check and turns the leaves purple; they are easily protected by cloches.

From late summer through to the new year there is a wide choice of cabbages, savoys, cauliflowers, red cabbage and brussels sprouts. Early sprouts, treated in exactly the same way as the summer cabbage, will start bearing early in September. Calabrese, a sort of green cauliflower, is a very useful additon to this galaxy. Sown in a bed in early May and transplanted in late June, it will produce its main head in August/September, and will then go on throwing out very palatable side shoots until the first frost.

There are several insect nuisances among which are the all too familiar cabbage white butterflies. The first generation in May/June is not as a rule serious, and it is not really worth while to try to eliminate them because their offspring will be heavily out-numbered by the invasion from the Continent in August. Claims are often made for the efficacy of companion and border plants as deterrents, but in many gardens they do not seem to afford a great deal of protection. The Large White conveniently lays its eggs in batches on the undersides of leaves; they are fairly easily spotted and destroyed. But the Small White eggs are laid singly and so are far less vulnerable. In a bad year one may have to resort to derris, though a solution of common salt in water can also be used. Even so it is difficult to get these sprays right into the growing points where much of the damage is done. Kieselguhr (diatomite) or very fine sand provide another

Vegetables planted in raised beds richly mulched with compost. This plan makes it easy to reach all parts of the bed for weeding and harvesting.
Photo: J. Anderson

alternative; they do not run off the leaves like a liquid spray, and their sharp grittiness upsets the caterpillar's metabolism.

The greyish brown creatures which burrow right into the hearts of cabbages and cauliflowers in July and August are larvae of the Cabbage Moth. To start with they feed on outer leaves and may be caught in the war against the Whites; later, there is no way of getting at them. But they pupate in the soil just below their host plant, so keep a look-out for them when clearing the old stumps.

Another very tiresome trouble is the purple-grey cabbage

aphid which makes its first visible appearance in mid-summer and continues its depredations until the first hard frost, but the more vigorous the plant the less likely it is to be affected. The eggs have overwintered on broccoli stems, and wingless 'stem mothers' emerge in late spring to start small colonies. After two or three wingless generations winged forms appear and this is where the damage begins. So the first preventative measure, if the aphids have been present the year before, is to uproot the old stems without waiting to harvest the last bits of greenstuff, and to chop them up quickly into the compost heap. From the end of June onwards make regular inspections for incipient colonies; their presence, if not obvious on upper leaf surfaces, is betrayed by discoloured patches and a curling of leaf edges. Red cabbage often seems to be their first choice, but all brassicas and other cruciferous species, such as swedes and shepherd's purse, are possible hosts. The colonies can be squashed in situ or cut out and burnt. Their powdery waxy coating makes them difficult to attack with sprays, and some individuals will even survive a heavy application of pyrethrum dust. Unfortunately they do not seem to be very attractive to predators; but some further suggestions for dealing with them are given in Chapter 19.

The larvae of the cabbage root fly are small white grubs which feed on the skin and young roots of all brassica species during the development stage soon after transplanting. Over-manuring increases the danger. Damage is most likely to occur on early summer plantings, and is first indicated by a wilting of the outer leaves during the hotter part of the day. Affected plants must be dug up at once with a ball of earth and shaken onto a flat surface so that the grubs can easily be collected and burned or fed to the robins. If caught early enough the plant can be put back into the soil at a greater depth than before with some extra compost, but it will never attain its full potentiality. There is no special bio-dynamic remedy; but if some plants have been lost from this cause in previous years and the garden is quite small, it is probably worth while to protect a dozen or so plants by fixing 10 cm (4 in) squares of roofing felt round the stems after transplanting. Make a hole in the centre of each square, and cut a slit to it from the middle of one side.

Clubroot is a fungus infection which causes large swellings on the roots, usually just below ground level. It may attack all species of the Cruciferae family, so mustard and rape should not be used for green manure on infested soil. It may start on seedlings while still in the seed bed, so be very careful with bought-in plants or any which may be cadged from neighbours. If it gets in during the development stage soon after transplanting, it can be a killer, but later infections on sprouts or broccoli are not so serious except for subsequent crops. With a sound crop rotation allowing at least three years between cruciferous crops it should not give much trouble. Although the spores may persist for seven years in some soils, regular treatment with bio-dynamic compost can eliminate them quite quickly provided that scrupulous attention is paid to the removal of all weeds which can carry the disease; some of these are shepherd's purse, charlock, wild radish, cuckoo flower and others.

THE LEGUMES

Broad Beans

They do not require a very rich soil, but they do appreciate some extra potash which can be given in the form of wood ash. Early establishment reduces the danger of later attack by blackfly. Some people in some districts are able to get a good stand from a late autumn sowing, but in other places the main shoots often die back and the side shoots springing from the hypocotyls may be rather weak, or they may not shoot at all. Owing to slow germination February and even March sowings are chancy if the soil is still cold, and many of the seeds are liable to rot. The remedy is to sow in deep boxes under protection at 5–7.5 cm (2–3 in) apart in January or February. The seedlings will develop a massive root system very quickly after they appear above the soil, so, if they are not planted out when four leaves have formed, it will be impossible to remove them from the box without extensive root damage. As they are quite hardy by then they can be planted out safely even in adverse weather conditions, but not of course into frozen ground.

There are now two or three strains of dwarfs in the seed catalogues, and some gardeners are so pleased with them that they have given up the older tall types altogether. Others have tried the dwarfs for a year or two and have rejected them. The dwarfs produce up to four stems per plant and are extremely prolific flowerers, but often the set is not as good as it might be. The proportion of bean to containing pod is higher than for talls, but the beans are smaller and not so easy to extract. New gardeners are advised to try both types for a year or two before deciding which suits them best.

Blackfly is the chief scourge of broad beans. The arrival of the first flies in May is often not immediately obvious, especially as many varieties have a small black spot at the base of the leaves; but it is betrayed by the black ants which feed on the excreted sugars. There is no record of the ants actually bringing the fly. Considerable though not complete protection is provided by regular weekly sprays of nettle *jauche* and/or seaweed from the time the plants are 23 cm (9 in) high, but as the leaves are very shiny on top, both the undersides and the soil must be sprayed: perhaps this makes the sap less attractive. The growing tips of the plants are pinched out as soon as the upper flowers are seen not to be setting; they make quite a good spinach if they are free of fly. Hover flies are the best predators on blackfly, but it is not easy to attract them at the critical time.

The leaves of maturing broad beans sometimes develop 'chocolate spot', a name which is fully descriptive. More often than not it is a sign that the plants cannot find all the potash they would like. If the spots are noticed soon after their first appearance they can be checked by the usual foliar sprays, but the trouble should not arise if the spraying programme mentioned above has been adopted and 501 has been used.

French Beans

For the elderly gardener french beans are a trial in that they bear their crop near the ground and harvesting involves a lot of painful stooping. But, compared with runner beans, their earlier maturity and superior flavour make the effort rewarding, and there are one or two excellent climbing varieties which will continue bearing until the first frost.

Sowing direct out of doors is chancy if there is still a serious risk of frost, but plants ready to go out in late May or early June can be raised under cover either in deep boxes or in soil blocks; small pots are not very suitable because the strong taproot is impeded even before the cotyledons emerge from the soil, but deep yoghourt pots with a hole pierced in the bottom make good seedling pots as they are deeper. In a heated greenhouse the May/June gap in the main garden can be bridged by a sowing in 20 cm (8 in) pots, three plants per pot, in February or early March. A sowing at the same time can be made in the tomato bed if carefully spaced; though the plant association is not ideal, a few welcome pickings can be had before the tomatoes get too big. The main stems of french beans tend to bend over sideways, with the result that some of the beans touch the soil and are extremely tempting to slugs. Strings or bushy twigs as supports get in the way of picking, but a couple of straight twigs close to each stem will help; earthing up the stems has also been recommended.

The seedlings before emergence are liable to attack by soil-dwelling nuisances which eat into the growing points and the undeveloped first pair of leaves, and they also nibble the cotyledons. The plants are either killed outright or else survive in such a weak and dishevelled condition that they are not worth retention. The chief culprit is the bean seed fly (*Delia platura*), but young slugs and the spotted snake millipede (*Blaniulus guttulatus*), together with a small white species of springtail, can all contribute to the damage. They are almost certainly attracted in the first place by manure or compost which was not fully rotted when dug in. If the trouble has been experienced in the past it is a good precaution to sow some extra seed alongside the main row or in a separate container for filling gaps. Broad beans and runners may also be similarly attacked but to a lesser degree.

Some gardeners like to plant french beans or similar types for their seed to be used as haricots during the winter; in this case it is essential to plant them as soon as possible because the later pods are slow to ripen and may be spoilt by an early frost. Also it is more than ever necessary to keep the pods off the ground, away from slugs and damp soil. Preparation 501 is given when the first batch of pods would normally be taken for use as a vegetable. For table use the spray would be applied soon after the first flowers have set.

Peas

Like runner beans, peas need some extra compost whatever crop they may be following in the rotation. The compost must be well rotted and, if it is in short supply, it can merely be lightly worked in down the lines of the drills. Experiments at the Vegetable Research Station have shown that from first flowering onwards peas need ample water for maximum yields, so in dry weather, unless they have been heavily mulched, irrigation can be beneficial. 501 is best used when the first flower buds are beginning to show.

There are many different varieties with quite a wide range in the time which it takes to come into flowering. By making a judicious selection it is possible to have peas for the kitchen from mid-May to late September. The first come from a quick-growing variety sown (in the Midlands) under cloches in January, and a longer-term type can be sown at the same time if sufficient cloches are available. As the plants can stand moderate frost, the cloches can be used for more sensitive crops when the peas are a few centimetres high and are ready for sticking. The last crop comes from an early variety sown in July, but this is liable to be attacked by mildew and may in some seasons require regular treatment with 501 and 508. Most modern varieties seem to have lost the potential to go on cropping over a sustained period and peter out disappointingly; but home-grown bio-dynamically treated seed from these same varieties behaves somewhat better. In this connection it is worth mentioning Dwarf Greensleeves (by no means dwarf!) because it produces a number of side shoots which prolong the cropping period.

There are several small creatures which like to get into the swelling pods, but the damage done is usually slight and there are no simple methods of prevention. A rather more serious nuisance is the pea weevil (*Sitonia lineatus*): it is seldom seen because it works at night and feeds on the leaf edges of young seedlings, giving them a scalloped appearance. Their larvae feed on the nodules and they also like broad beans. The only way to attack them is to apply derris or pyrethrum dust late in the evening; but there is some evidence to show that a light mulch of lawn mowings spread over the rows after sowing can give some protection. Strong healthy seedlings soon grow away from any damage, but weaklings may never recover.

Runner Beans

These are one of the most rewarding and prolific crops for the home garden, but from a rotational point of view they have the disadvantage of requiring tall poles or canes which, even when arranged as tripods, can cause undesirable shade on adjoining crops. They can, however, be grown for several years in succession on a small, carefully selected plot without deterioration, the shade being cast on a pathway or hedge. The plot will need a good annual dressing of compost, for although the beans produce most of their own nitrogen, they must have an extensive root system to meet their heavy water requirements. A generous straw mulch will prevent evaporation from the soil and will reduce soil compaction due to frequent treading during harvest. The plants are susceptible to frost damage; on evenings when a frost is expected a late spray of 507 may give some protection. For an early crop a few seeds can be sown in a deep box and transplanted when the first pair of leaves is fully developed.

If blackfly should make an appearance they will have to be tackled early with foliar sprays and perhaps even with an insecticide. But it would be worthwhile also to look back and see whether an unwise cultural operation may have made the plants more susceptible to attack. Perhaps manure in too raw a state has been dug in, or possibly one may have followed the advice to bury kitchen waste and old brassica stems in the bean trench during the winter, with adverse effects on the constitution of the sap. Failure of the flowers to set or a tendency to drop off without opening can happen, especially in dry weather. Careful inspection will usually reveal a small hole at the base of the flower. It is made by the small bumblebee which normally pollinates the flowers; it is looking for the nectar which has been prematurely produced before a delayed opening of the flower, and in making the hole it cuts through the sheath which carries the anthers. Consequently, even if the flower does open, no pollen is formed and the ovaries are not fertilised. Spraying the plants, and especially the flowering stalks, with plain water in late evening or early morning will help to cure the trouble.

ROOT CROPS

Beetroot

It is often implied in gardening books and articles that beetroot following a heavily composted crop such as a brassica will not need any further manuring; this may be true for some very fertile soils, but not as a general rule. Beet seedlings like some well rotted sifted compost in the drills to get them off to a good start; the strong seedlings can then utilise to the full the residual fertility for their further growth. It is not advisable to sow beetroot before April. Earlier sowings tend to bolt, but there is a comparatively new variety which does not succumb to this tendency.

There are three different types—globe, cylindrical and the old long tapering sort which has now gone quite out of favour. The cylindrical varieties make tall, well grown roots which are very convenient for slicing, but some do not have the full flavour of the globes.

A late crop can profitably be sown in July, perhaps after early potatoes. It is not generally known that beetroot can be successfully transplanted; in addition to thinnings, seedlings for transplanting can be raised in a deep box. The best stage to move them is when four to six leaves have been formed, but it is advisable to remove the two largest of these before planting out in order to reduce transpiration while new root hairs are developing.

In some districts the young emerging seedlings are especially attractive to sparrows which will strip a row very quickly. They can be stopped by a single strand of black cotton stretched a few centimetres directly above the rows. Young seedlings are also susceptible to 'black-leg', a true description of a disease which kills them off before they have had a chance to develop beyond the cotyledon stage. The disease usually only appears when seed has been sown in cold soil with insufficient nourishment; so it can be prevented by creating a good tilth, putting some well rotted compost in the drills and exercising a little patience. If there is an urgent need for early beet, the best course is to sow some seed under protection and transplant later.

Carrots

The lighter types of soil with a high proportion of sand are best for carrots, but the stump-rooted varieties will give perfectly good results even on heavy clays provided that the soil has been worked up into a sound state of fertility and structure. The seed needs to be sown in a finely worked bed at 1 cm (½ in) deep: after covering, the drills are gently firmed with the back of the rake to get rid of any puffiness. It is all too easy to sow the small seed more thickly than is either necessary or desirable. The use of 'chitted' or 'pelleted' seed reduces the task of thinning. An early crop from a quick growing variety can be obtained by sowing in a cold frame in February or March; they will be finished before the frame is needed later on for melons or cucumbers. It is rarely worth sowing in the open before April and the main crop for winter storage is best left until late May or early June when it has the greatest chance of escaping the attention of the carrot fly. Carrots can follow a heavily manured brassica crop without any further additions to the soil apart from a spray of 500; if a little extra compost is deemed necessary, it must be given in a very well rotted condition, for otherwise the roots are inclined to fork. Preparation 501 is used on carrots in the evening when the roots are starting to swell, and again on the main crop two to three weeks before harvest. Harvest should not be delayed beyond early October in the hope that, if left longer, the roots will put on a little more weight; they are much more likely to crack open, making them more difficult to clean in the kitchen and more liable to rot during storage.

In most districts the curse of the carrot grower is the root fly which also lives on the roots of wild Umbelliferae in the hedgerows. It is a very small fly and it is almost impossible to observe it on the wing. Although its life history is well known, no research seems to have been done to discover why, like the celery fly, it flourishes more in some years than in others, nor are there any traditional explanations for this phenomenon. The first generation hatches from its overwintering pupae in the soil quite early in the season, and the larvae start feeding on even the smallest vestiges of roots, announcing their presence by a bronzing of the leaves which soon wilt and die. There is usually a gap between mid-May and mid-June before the second generation gets busy, and they will continue to give trouble until late autumn when they also feed on parsnips, parsley roots and the various winter radishes.

No reliable biological or cultural deterrent has yet been discovered, though many and varied are the devices which have been tried, nor are there any generally known predators. The adults are reputed to be attracted by the scent of carrots, particularly from seedlings bruised during thinning, and are also drawn to soil that has been manured too recently. Carrots like mature soil, at least two years distant from manuring, but some well-ripened compost is all right if needed. Sow thinly to avoid having to disturb the soil by thinning. No 'jamming' device, such as tarred string or companion planting with onions or garlic, has as yet proved entirely effective: nor has it ever been surmised what attracts them to parsnips and radishes. On a very small scale it is reported that a barrier of 23 cm (9 in) black polythene strip erected round the plot will defeat their low flying habit. Block planting by broadcasting the seed over a rectangular patch so that only the outer plants are attacked does not always work; not a single edible root was harvested from a patch measuring 150 cm by 90 cm (5 ft by 3 ft). The main hope for the future lies in finding a cultural or homoeopathic way of making the plants less attractive to the fly. (See Chapter 19).

Celeriac

Although not widely grown and only rarely seen in the shops, celeriac is a very useful and palatable vegetable for the autumn and winter, both grated raw, in soups and stews, or served with a white sauce. For the best results it needs to be out in its final position by the end of June. Seed is sown in pans in March, preferably with some heat; the very small seeds are thinly sprinkled on the surface of the potting compost and only just covered with fine sand to allow a modicum of light to reach the seed. As soon as two true leaves have formed the seedlings are pricked out into boxes at least 7.5 cm (3 in) deep filled with a rich potting compost. Though they are still very small they are not difficult to handle as they will already have a well branched root system: they are spaced at not less than 6 cm (2½ in) apart. At transplanting they will need quite large holes, spaced at 30 cm by 45 cm (12 in by 18 in), for their mass of roots to be fully spread out. When the plants are established a mulch of leaf-mould will retain moisture for the surface roots.

Celeriac is quite a greedy feeder and responds to a generous application of well rotted manure (in preference to compost) worked into the bed shortly before transplanting. Some gardeners like to remove the lower leaves at least once during the growing season, but comparative observations, leaving some plants alone and removing leaves from others, suggest that this back-breaking operation is not necessary. In some seasons an appreciable number of plants will bolt. The precise reason is not known, but it does not seem to be a day-length phenomenon due to planting too early, and is probably caused by dry weather in July. This tendency must be borne in mind when planning for 501; on no account should it be sprayed before the roots have started to swell. Bolted plants are useless except perhaps for soup, and are best removed at once. The plants will tolerate a little frost, but a hard one will damage them, so it is best to clear the plot in November. When harvesting, instead of digging up the whole plants, it is easier to cut round and under the bulbs with a large knife, leaving the rootlets in the ground where they are greatly appreciated by the earth worms. The larger leaves are pulled off and the small ones cut just above the growing point. The latter can be dried in a slow oven and kept for flavouring soups.

The celery fly or leaf miner can be serious trouble in some years and it may even start on the seedlings in the boxes. The small flies emerge in April/May from their pupae which have over-wintered in the soil. After mating the eggs are laid on the underside of the leaves and the larvae immediately burrow in to feed on the green cells between the two skins of the leaves. Their presence is soon obvious from the curly white patterns which they make. The larvae take about three weeks to mature and then pupate either in the soil or in the leaves themselves. The second generation begins to get busy from late June onwards. All cultivated species of the Umbelliferae family are vulnerable, but attacks are spasmodic. For instance, in 1979, after seriously damaging celeriac, celery, parsnips, lovage and angelica, larvae were found in the fine foliage of carrots and caraway; but in 1980 damage was negligible. Very often the first signs of attack appear on lovage, so it is advisable to keep a keen watch on any lovage or angelica plants there may be in the garden from early May onwards; the next crop likely to be affected is parsnips. On a small scale infested leaves or portions of leaf can be removed and burned; but in a large garden there are difficulties because the tough leaf skins prevent penetration by insecticides, though nicotine is reported to be effective. If the trouble has been present during the summer it is worth lightly forking the soil round the lovage and other plants once or twice in the autumn and winter in the hope that birds will find the overwintering pupae.

Florence Fennel

For those who appreciate the flavour of fennel the bulbous-rooted variety known as Florence Fennel or Finocchio provides an interesting addition to the menu. Like the leek it is not a true root but a kind of bulb developing at ground level on the top of a strong taproot, and formed by the swollen bases of the leaf sheaths. It is a greedy crop and must be sown on soil which has been given a generous application of well rotted compost (or manure). The seed catalogues recommend successional sowings from mid-May onwards, but sometimes sowings made before mid-summer run straight to seed without forming bulbs. This tendency has also been observed in later sowings which have received a check or which have not been given as much compost as they would like. A good spacing is 23 cm by 30 cm (9 in by 12 in) and it is easier to make spot sowings at this spacing than to sow thinly in drills. The bulbs may be earthed up for blanching when they start to swell, but this is not essential. Apart from the bolting habit which could perhaps be checked by judicious use of 501, there is little to worry about in the way of unfriendly insects or diseases. Except perhaps in the extreme south, one should not expect to grow bulbs as large as those sometimes found in the shops—they are imported.

Leeks

Although strictly speaking the edible part of a leek consists of blanched leaf sheaths, they are treated here as roots because they develop below soil level and they fit into the root break of the crop rotation. They like a deep, fairly rich soil, so some compost or manure is dug into the bed a week or two before planting out, but this is not necessary if they are following well manured early potatoes. The compost need not be fully rotted as it has to supply nutrients over quite a long period.

The seed is normally sown in an open bed in April or early May; but in a cold year or in soils that are slow to warm up germination may be delayed and patchy, and the seedlings may not be quite strong enough for the ideal planting time in June or early July. To overcome this difficulty a March or early April sowing can be made in a frame. Another way is to sow the seed in a tray in a warm greenhouse during March. When the seedlings are about 5 cm (2 in) high in April they are taken up in little clumps of half a dozen or so and spaced out in a well composted furrow outside or in a cold frame: by mid-June there will be plenty of fine, strong seedlings. But if the crop is to follow summer brassicas or another crop coming off in August, an outside sowing in mid-May is sufficient.

The usually recommended spacing for planting out is 23 cm (9 in) apart with 45 cm (18 in) between rows, but these distances can be appreciably reduced if need be. The seedlings used to be planted in a trench like celery, but this method is now seldom used except to produce giants for flower shows. Holes about 20 cm (8 in) deep are made with a dibber or with a crowbar if the soil is hard. But a 180 cm (6 ft) length of 3 cm (1½ in) piping is very easy to handle and its blunt end avoids the danger of leaving an air space at the bottom of the holes. The seedlings are pushed or dropped into the holes as far as they will go, if necessary trimming the longest roots. The usual practice is then to fill each hole with water which will wash down enough soil to cover the roots. A little sifted compost in each hole before watering is an improvement, better still if gently firmed with a stick. Although some authorities disagree, it is important that the seedlings are large enough for at least 5–7.5 cm (2–3 in) of leaf to project above soil level: the holes are soon filled by rain wash and hoeing, so shorter seedlings may get buried and will not be able to force their way up. Subsequently a mulch will help to control weeds and avoid crust formation. Preparation 501 is sprayed at any time after full growth has started and when other crops are being treated.

Leeks suffer from very few troubles. Some gardeners like to cut back the larger leaves from time to time to prevent fungus attack from the soil (and to stimulate growth in the young leaves). Occasionally a pink rot develops in the stem, working inwards from the outside, but there is no remedy once it has started.

Onions and Shallots

Some experts keep a special bed for onions, building up a deep friable topsoil over several years, and not moving on until there are signs that diseases may be developing. This is not a practice to be recommended because it makes a very unbalanced demand on the productive forces of that particular plot, and the disharmony could well affect adjoining crops. So it is better to include the onions in the root break of a rotation, but they do appreciate rather more compost than most other root crops.

By far the easiest way to grow onions is to buy sets and plant them in March/April. But some bio-dynamic gardeners may object to this method because the sets are produced abroad under very artificial conditions: they will grow their crop from seed sown either in mid-August or mid-April. In the former case a bed is chosen in a sheltered spot and the seedlings are left alone during the winter; in March or early April they are transplanted to their final position in the same way as for sets. In the case of direct sowing in the spring, the seedlings are thinned out when 10–15 cm (4–6 in) high, and the thinnings are used for salads; the young seedlings in bad areas may be decimated by the onion fly which can, however, be warded off by sprinkling a few carrot seeds in the drills. An onion seed bed has to be worked to a very fine tilth but the drills must be very firm; this can be done simply by pressing hard with the back of a rake or even by laying a thin pole along the line of the drill and treading on it.

Before deciding on the best spacing for the crop it is as well to consult the person who will use the onions. Many seem to prefer a medium size 7.5–10 cm (3–4 in) in diameter which means that they can be spaced in the row at not more than 12.5 cm (5 in) apart. But if big fat ones are preferred they will have to go in at 20–23 cm (8–9 in) between each set or seedling. In any year a few onions will probably bolt, throwing up a flowering stem from the side of the main bulb; some years are worse than others. The stems should be cut off as close to the ground as possible and the bulbs will go on developing, but the bases of the stems eventually die back, turn brown and start a rot which will spread to the bulbs if stored; so the best plan with bolters is to get them into the kitchen as soon as possible. A spray of 501 in early June would help to check this tendency.

Neck rot is a trouble which needs attention. It is a fungus which may get into the necks when the bulbs are beginning to ripen after attaining full growth; it develops later in storage and

Bio-dynamic techniques produce excellent results in flower borders also.
Photo: J. Anderson

will destroy whole bulbs if they have not been thoroughly dried before being put away. Large bulbs are more vulnerable than small ones. If August is cloudy and damp a preventative spray of 508 and perhaps another application of 501 are advisable. The standard advice to bend the tops over early in August to promote ripening is sound enough in a hot dry year: in less favourable weather the practice is more likely to promote neck rot: in any case the tops will bend over of their own accord when they are ready.

Some people prefer shallots to onions as their flavour is not so pungent. They are one of the easiest crops to grow and do not suffer from any serious pests or disease. Moreover, once they have been grown for the first time, there is no need to buy sets again; some of the crop can always be kept for planting in the following year. They respond to a moderate application of compost, and will only produce rather small bulbs if treated stingily.

Purchased sets are usually large and will give up to a dozen bulbs at harvest if planted at 23 cm (9 in) apart in the row and 30 cm (12 in) between rows in March. A lesser known practice is to plant the babies which are too small for convenient kitchen use; they can be spaced as close as 7.5 cm by 7.5 cm (3 in by 3 in) and each will yield at least a couple of good-sized bulbs. Like onions they must be thoroughly dried and ripened before being stored as they too can develop neck rot.

Parsnips

Parsnip seed is one of the slowest to germinate; even under the best conditions it will take a fortnight or more to come through the soil. If sown in cold or sticky soil there is a good chance that most of the seed will rot, and there is no bio-dynamic treatment which will avert this fate. So it is as well to disregard the advice on the seed packet to sow in March. Although later sowings are rather slow to swell, perfectly good medium-sized roots can be obtained from sowing as late as mid-May.

Parsnips are not a demanding crop; they will be quite happy following a well treated crop of brussels sprouts or winter cabbage, especially if given a little finely sifted compost in the drills to get them well started. A week or two before sowing the plot is given a light cultivation, weeds are removed, and 500 is sprayed if that has not been done earlier. The cultivation will help the soil to warm up and dry out a little. Seed is sown in drills at 30 cm (12 in) apart after working up a fine tilth, but the seedlings will need thinning later on and it can be very aggravating to find the best ones in the wrong place. This can be avoided by spot sowing; holes are made with the leek dibber to the same depth and spaced at 15–20 cm (6–8 in) in the rows. The holes are filled with a seed compost (see pp. 78–9) making sure that no air gaps are left at the bottom and leaving 2.5 cm (1 in) at the tops. Three or four seeds are sown in each hole, and the holes are filled by raking over the bed. Each station is thinned to one seedling only as soon as the strongest ones have asserted themselves. This method generally prevents the formation of forked roots. To fit in with other sprayings 501 can be used at any time after half a dozen strong leaves have developed.

Parsnips are liable to suffer from canker, those all too familiar brown blotches on the roots which sometimes develop into deep pits. They are caused by micro-organisms which get into roots damaged by hoeing, and also into cracks in the skin which may appear when the root is swelling too quickly or grows against a sharp fragment of grit in the soil. There is no treatment other than care in hoeing and creating a good tilth originally.

The other main trouble is the celery leaf miner which can be devastating in a bad year. A full description is given under celeriac.

Potatoes

As explained in Chapter 8, potatoes need a break of their own in a rotation, but this is seldom possible or worthwhile in a small garden; a few earlies for a treat can usually be fitted into the root break. It is essential to start off with sound seed tubers taken from virus-free plants. In most parts of the country it is risky to use one's own seed for more than one season; for, even though a tuber may look clean and sound, by the second year it will probably have been tainted by virus and will not yield so well as a similar one bought in. Home-saved seed is best selected at harvest time, choosing clean small to medium sized tubers. These are stored separately, covered over in a cool, dry and frost-free place: or they can be buried in crocks with at least 15 cm (6 in) of soil on the top; they are taken up for chitting at the end of February. This exposure to the winter earth forces produces a plant with strong upright growth quite distinct from that of stored seed; the yield is slightly improved, but there is no information as to whether the quality is enhanced.

Home-grown seed can, however, be produced by growing a few plants from eyes which dodge the virus. In March dormant eyes are selected from the centre or basal end of sound tubers, not from the 'rose' where most of the eyes or buds are situated; the latter more often than not will turn into miserable short-lived plants with a few tubers the size of marbles. They are cut out with a very small wedge of tuber and planted under cover like seeds 5 cm (2 in) apart in a tray with at least a 5 cm (2 in) depth of soil. They are hardened off at the five to six leaf stage, and are planted out in May in shallow depressions to allow for future earthing up. In loamy, chalky or clay soils it is useful to strengthen the silica forces by distributing some coarse sand or broken quartz in the bottom of the planting holes. It is very important to keep these plants free from the aphids which carry the virus, so a careful watch must be kept for them and as a preventative measure nettle *jauche* can be sprayed every ten days. An evening spray of 501 is applied when the haulm is in full growth and again when the first signs of leaf yellowing appear.

Seed potatoes are usually chitted before planting. In early March they are put on end into trays or boxes with the roses upwards, and are exposed to strong light (but not direct sunlight) at temperatures between 8–13°C (45–55°F). The eyes develop into short stumpy growths which come on quickly when planted out, and so planting can be delayed until there is less danger from late frosts. Before planting, the weaker eyes are rubbed off, leaving not more than three per tuber; larger tubers with a lot of strong eyes can be cut in pieces to give two or three sets. Planting can be done either in holes made with a trowel or else in furrows or trenches which may be taken out mechanically in larger gardens; they must be deep enough for 7.5 cm (3 in) of soil to cover the top shoots after planting. The choice of method will depend to a certain extent on the previous cultivations. Following a fertility building crop dibbling is less laborious on a small scale; but if compost or manure has to be given (potatoes respond to heavy dressings), it can be put in the planting trenches. Most of the new crop will be borne on root-like shoots arising from the base of the original eye, but these bearing shoots can also come from the underground nodes of the young stems. It therefore pays to have a good covering of soil over the set, or else to earth up the rows as soon as the first leaves appear above ground. One of the advantages of chitting is that the nodes have already started to form in the compact shoots and will be more closely spaced on the stems after planting than is the case with an unchitted seed tuber.

The chief cause for worry in a potato crop is blight, a fungal disease which first appears on the leaves as brown patches soon turning black and destroying the whole leaf; the spores then fall onto the soil and will infect the tubers so that they rot either before or soon after harvest. It is not to be confused with viral symptoms or stem rot whose dark patches do not enlarge so quickly, do not turn black and do not have the typical furry spore growth on the under sides of the leaves Blight seldom appears before mid-July, more often in August, so the early crop generally escapes. The first precaution is the normal spray of 501, given in the evening when flower buds can be seen at ends of the stems; this is the time when the new tubers begin to swell. Some silica given at planting time, as described for eyes, is an additional measure. Then if conditions are damp and sultry, silica must again be called in, both in the form of equisetum tea and as a dust of diatomite or a dilute solution (1 per cent) of waterglass. If in spite of all precautions the disease gets a hold, the only course left is to cut all the haulms at ground level and leave what crop there is to ripen off in the soil. A confident compost maker can safely put the diseased haulms into the middle of a heap in the sure knowledge that the micro-life in the heap, assisted by the compost preparations, will deal with the fungus spores. But a less confident operator may consider it safer to burn the haulms. Avoid hoeing on 'leaf-days' or moon perigee as this encourages fungal development followed by blight.

Another far less serious trouble is scab, forming brown blistery blotches on the skins of the tubers; they are unsightly but do not penetrate into the flesh or impair cooking quality. It is thought that the fungus gains entry through scratches on the skin when swelling tubers rub against sharp particles in the soil, but this is by no means certain and there are probably other factors involved. For instance, it has been noticed that potatoes planted over a recent bonfire site suffer more severely than their neighbours. It is more prevalent on alkaline soils than on those on the acid side.

Sometimes on an occasional plant the upper leaflets start to curl inwards, then they turn yellow with dark purple patches and the bases of the stems decay into a black slimy mass; the trouble does not necessarily infect every stem on a plant. The disease is known as 'black leg' and is usually carried on the seed tubers. Although it does not spread to neighbouring plants, it is best to remove any which begin to show the symptoms as soon as possible. The tubers at this stage are quite edible, but on no account should they be put into store because it is here that the guilty bacteria really get busy and infect healthy tubers.

Curled leaves are also a symptom of the commonest potato virus disease—potato leaf roll—but in this case the lower leaves are the first to curl up. The other very common and more serious virus is merely called 'virus Y'; here the plants become stunted, and the leaves get smaller and puckered with a yellowish mottling. Once plants have become infected with either of these viruses there is no known way of curing them. The only protection against them is to buy seed from a reliable source, and on a small scale to keep an eye open for greenfly on the young shoots; they are the carriers of both viruses and can be dealt with by spraying fresh nettle *jauche*.

Finally, if one is moving to an established garden which has been treated conventionally in the past, there is a possibility that the soil may be infected with potato eelworm cysts. If so, many potato plants will turn yellow and die prematurely, however well they have been treated with manure. There is no sure remedy and the usual advice is to keep the infected land free of potatoes (and tomatoes) for at least six years. The cysts can be seen with the aid of a hand lens as small pustules on the roots of infected plants. Once the worms have been awakened from the cysts by the scent of a potato plant they are great travellers; they are so small that a journey of 2.5 millimetres is equivalent to a human walk of five kilometres.

Swedes, Turnips and Kohl Rabi

Between them these three will provide a root crop for most of the year. Strictly speaking, kohl rabi is not a root but a swollen stem, but for those who follow moon rhythms it must be worked on root days.

The summer varieties of turnip are fairly hardy and can be sown in March for use in May/June; small successional sowings at three-week intervals are better than one large one. They need quite a rich soil to keep them moving and prevent them from turning 'woody'. Different varieties are better for winter storage and are sown in July/August; they are not entirely frost-hardy and any remaining in the ground at the end of October should be taken up for safety and put into store.

Swedes are more of an autumn and winter crop for which purpose they are ideally sown in June, but July sowing is quite satisfactory. Spaced at about 15 cm (6 in) apart after thinning, they will not grow too large and become coarse. They are very hardy and will stand all through the winter to be cropped when needed, but pigeons are particularly fond of their tops in hard weather and may have to be deterred.

Kohl rabi is in a different category in that it can conveniently be sown in a seed bed, the seedlings being transplanted to their final positions at 30 cm by 38 cm (12 in by 15 in) when they have two or three well formed leaves. They are best eaten when they reach tennis ball size, before they get stringy. Successional sowings can be made from mid-April until July, but they are not so hardy as swedes and do not keep very well in storage.

Preparation 501 is given as a morning spray to all these crops when they first begin to swell. They are all liable to clubroot attack; but although they are not seriously affected by the fungus, they do prolong its presence in an infected soil, and it is therefore unwise to plant them in places where the disease has appeared in recent brassica crops.

LEAF AND SALAD CROPS

Corn Salad (Lamb's Lettuce)

It is hardly worth growing this crop during the months when lettuce is plentiful, but it does come in very handy for greening a salad during the colder parts of the year as it is frost-hardy. Sown in September in rows 15 cm (6 in) apart, or even broadcast, the thinnings will be ready for use six weeks later. Then the main plants at 4 in. apart can be cropped during the winter. Another sowing can be made during March, but these plants may run to seed rather quickly. Once established it will usually sow itself freely.

Cress

If grown as a crop and not just in punnets or similar receptacles, a sowing of cress will provide several cuts before it starts running to seed. A patch of 0.37–0.46 sq. m (4–5 sq. ft) will give a cut for two people nearly every day for a month or more; by the time one has cut over the whole area the first part will have made enough leaf for the second cut to be started. It is usually possible to get at least four cuts. The patch is worked to a fine tilth with some well rotted compost; the seed is scattered as evenly as possible (but not too thickly) over the surface and is lightly covered with some of the soil which has been put aside for the purpose. Any variety of cress can be treated in this way, but Dobies Super Salad is perhaps the best.

Endive

Though not particularly suitable for a very small garden, it is strange that endive is not more widely grown in Britain when there is adequate space available. Being fairly hardy it is most useful as a green salad crop for the autumn and early winter when lettuce is becoming more difficult. It is sown thinly in shallow drills 30 cm (12 in) apart in July or August after the earlier peas or potatoes have come off the ground. Some fine compost along the drills will give the seedlings a good start; they are thinned to 23 cm (9 in) apart in the row when they have about four leaves. When grown at this time of the year endive does not bolt, so 501 can be given two to three weeks after thinning. The green leaves are rather bitter to the taste, but when blanched they are sweet, with a more pronounced flavour than lettuce. Blanching can be achieved by inverting a 15 cm (6 in) pot or similar utensil over each plant and blocking up any holes which might admit light; it is better to do only a few plants at a time, moving the pots onto others as harvesting proceeds. Another method is to gather up all the outer leaves and tie them round the hearts; it is easier to have the ties prepared in advance so that they can be slipped over the gathered leaves. The latter method has the disadvantage that the bruised leaves may provide an entry for botrytis mould.

Slugs are the worst enemy. Not only do they enjoy the blanched leaves, but they also seem to think that the compact protected hearts would make an ideal wintering place. Moreover most of them cannot be enticed out of the hearts by any kind of bait or pellet. The only way to deal with the menace is to try at an early stage to prevent them from getting in, perhaps by covering the ground with soot, ashes or pine needles.

Lettuce

If one has a greenhouse (not necessarily heated), a cold frame or cloches, lettuce for the table can be grown all the year round by a judicious choice of varieties; those which have been specially bred to grow through the winter will run straight to flower if sown in the spring. Sugar Cos, also known as Little Gem, seems to be an exception to this rule, for if sown in September or October it will continue to make slow growth under cloches or in a frame and, slugs permitting, will provide tasty though small heads from December onwards. All the same, unless one is a lettuce fiend, it is probably not worth a small gardener's time to struggle with an out-of-season crop of this nature.

There are many different types and varieties of lettuce, and the choice is largely a personal one. Some people prefer the 'butterhead' kind most commonly sold in the shops; others like the 'crispheads' of which the large Webb's Wonderful is the chief representative; still others seldom grow anything except

Sugar Cos which, in addition to its excellent flavour and crispness, has the advantage that it can be planted more closely on account of its erect habit.

From April onwards three-weekly sowings can be made outside to provide a succession right through the season. But if one is a strict follower of the moon rhythms as described by Maria Thun, the gap between sowings must be monthly when the moon stands in the Fishes. Direct sowing with subsequent thinning is the normal practice; the plants receive no check and reach maturity more rapidly than transplants. But for a small garden there is quite a lot to be said for sowing very thinly in pans under protection: after hardening off the seedlings are transplanted at the four-leaf stage. A refinement is to transplant to soil blocks as soon as the seedlings can be conveniently handled; they will then go out to their final stations without check. The great advantage of adopting a transplanting technique, however, lies in the fact that one does not have to look around every two to three weeks for a spare patch to take the next sowing. Pan and block grown seedlings can nearly always find a home as a catch crop during the early stages of a widely spaced main crop. For example they can go between onion sets or shallots in March or early April. Later there will be almost certainly be room among newly transplanted brassicas, and there are several other situations which offer possibilities—a new strawberry bed, for instance.

Although not a greedy crop, lettuce does need a certain amount of well rotted compost, even if it follows a crop which has been heavily treated. If transplanted as a catch crop among other plants it will get all that it needs. Starved plants will usually bolt very quickly without making hearts, and so will plants treated with preparation 501 if it is applied too soon. But 501 given when hearts have started to form will stimulate the process and enhance the flavour.

Apart from sparrows, slugs and cutworms a possible worry is botrytis mould which may develop as a result of humid weather conditions or from over-generous manuring; it is also a serious danger in out-of-season crops at the back end of the year. It usually starts as brown patches on the midribs of the older leaves and spreads inwards to the heart; eventually the whole plant disintegrates to a mouldy mess. The use of 501 assists in warding off attack, but if conditions are muggy it may have to be supplemented by regular use of 508. If the disease does appear it is more than likely that an imbalance in the soil is responsible, perhaps due to raw manure, so the wise gardener will ask himself what he might have done wrong and will avoid the mistake in the future.

Collectively cutworms are caterpillars which later turn into two or three different species of moth; they spend the last part of their lives in the soil before pupating. They are very choosy in their diet and only eat the parts of seedlings just below the ground, so most of the leafy parts are left to wilt on the surface. This method of attack is quite different from slugs and is easily spotted. The culprit is usually found by scratching around in the few centimetres of soil near to the ruined plant or plants.

Radishes

In the Midlands it is seldom worth sowing radishes outside before mid-April: earlier sowings struggle along slowly and rarely produce the succulent roots obtained from quick growth. They can, however, give good results if sown in a cold frame from February onwards. As they germinate very quickly they are useful as 'markers' when sown very thinly in carrot, parsnip, onion and beetroot drills, making hoeing easier and providing some protection against sparrows in the case of beetroot. Using them in this way avoids having to find a special place for them. Later on, when grown as a sole crop, it is best to sow them in shallow drills 10 cm (4 in) wide, or even to broadcast them over several square centimetres. Push the top centimetre (½ in), of well worked soil to the sides, scatter the seed thinly and then cover over. In this country radishes respond more markedly than some other crops to the moon influences; even if on some occasions there is not a great deal of difference in the outward appearance of the roots sown in different constellations, those sown on root days have a distinctly better flavour.

Spinach

The so-called 'round' spinach (because its seeds are round) is a useful crop for spring and early summer when other vegetables are rather scarce. There are two types, both of which will often come out of the same named seed packet: one has dark green rounded leaves, the other paler and thinner arrow-shaped leaves, but there is not much difference in their performance. Spinach needs to be grown quickly for the best results, so it should be sown in a warm sunny place (or in a frame) with a good dressing of compost. It takes about five weeks to produce the first large leaves, though thinnings can be used in salads earlier; it will crop for about three weeks before running to seed. Successional sowings should therefore be made every three weeks for a regular supply. Cold starved plants will not produce any leaves worth picking before they bolt, and sowings made when the days begin to get shorter will also bolt very quickly.

Spinach Beet or Leaf Beet

Again there are two distinct types, but the seeds are marketed separately, one usually under the name Swiss Chard, whose wide white midribs can be separated from the green leaf and cooked like seakale. The other type is often called perpetual spinach, but this is a misnomer because it is a biennial. They can both be sown from May onwards and will be ready for cropping about ten weeks later. Swiss Chard stays rather dormant during the winter and may be killed by severe frost, but the perpetual continues to grow slowly and provides regular pickings. In the spring both put on a spurt of growth before running to seed in May/June.

Watercress

Contrary to its name, watercress does not necessarily have to be grown in water; it can in fact be planted successfully on a bed even in the more humid parts of the tropics. It will, however, require regular watering in dry weather, so it is best to plant it in a shallow depression, or even in a box outside the back door. As it will be cropped several times before it begins to flower, it needs a plentiful supply of compost to start with. It can be grown from the rooting stalks usually found when bought from a shop, but it is better to start it from seed which is sown in a pan, the seedlings being pricked out into their final positions at 15–23 cm (6–9 in) apart when they reach the four to five leaf stage.

Winter Radishes

The ordinary radish does not do so well once the days have begun to shorten, but there are three types of large radish which do not suffer from this disability; in fact they run to seed if sown before midsummer. They can therefore be conveniently grown when other spring crops have been harvested.

The Spanish Black radish attains tennis ball size or larger within ten weeks of sowing. They can be left in the ground until needed, but any roots remaining at the end of October are best lifted and stored in the same way as carrots. They are excellent for grating in salads and can also be cut into thin slices for nibbling.

China Rose is more cylindrical in habit; it is inclined to be unshapely with a wrinkled surface, and is more liable to attack by carrot root fly which causes brown patches and stains in the flesh. It is treated in the same way as Spanish Black but is milder in flavour.

Mino Early, a variety that has fallen out of favour and is at present unavailable, is rather like a greatly elongated turnip with half its cylindrical root in the soil and half above. It is a very rapid grower and its 3 cm (1½ in) diameter smooth white roots may reach a length of 30 cm (12 in).

Although it can be eaten raw, it is perhaps better cooked like turnips.

FRUIT CROPS

Cucumbers

Even in a small garden one or two ridge cucumber plants can be grown outside without encroaching on precious space, and will give quite a plentiful supply of somewhat small fruit in August and September. The name 'ridge' implies that the fruit have more pronounced ridges than the hothouse types, not that they have to be grown on ridges. Although the normal practice is to let them spread over the ground, they can easily be trained on an upright frame, wide mesh wirenetting or stout peasticks. The seeds are sown singly in 7.5 cm (3 in) pots or soil blocks under cover in early May and the plants are ready to go out four to five weeks later when they reach the five-leaf stage. The growing points of the seedlings are pinched out to leave four leaves from which branches will arise. The tips of these branches are again pinched out when they are about 23 cm (9 in) long; although they would eventually produce fruit, most of the fruit is borne on tertiary shoots.

Cucumbers are rather greedy, so the bed should be prepared with plenty of thoroughly rotted compost or manure. Quite a thick mulch is needed because most of the roots are close to the surface; without a mulch regular watering (which is essential) will soon wash the soil off the roots, but with a thick mulch moisture is retained and less watering is required in dry weather. Some judgement is necessary as to the right time to pick the fruit; if left to get too old, the seeds will have started to harden; but if taken too early, the flesh is inclined to be bitter. French beans are known to be a good companion plant for cucumbers.

A rarer type for out of doors, not found in most seed catalogues, is the apple cucumber. It is not so suitable for growing on a framework as the ridge type, but it is very prolific and does not require such detailed pinching out. It produces roundish pale green to white fruits not quite as large as a tennis ball, but their flavour is excellent and they are reputed to be innocuous for those who cannot easily digest the other types. The cultural treatment is the same as for ridge varieties.

Marrows

Under this heading are included the true marrows, courgettes, zucchinis (not a true courgette), pumpkins and squashes. There are two types—bush and trailing—but they all have similar characteristics and cultural requirements. The traditional method is to plant them on old rubbish heaps and half-burnt bonfire sites, but such places are not likely to be around in a bio-dynamic garden, and it is unwise to plant them on the top of a compost heap. Trailing types, however, can usefully be put at the base of a compost heap where their large leaves will provide shade for the heap and their straggling habit will not interfere with other crops. All the marrows are very tender and cannot withstand even a trace of frost. It is therefore advisable to sow them (with the round edge of the seed upwards) in 7.5 cm (3 in) pots under cover for transplanting in late May or June. If planted out earlier it is a sensible precaution to have some form of protection handy for each plant in case frost is threatened.

Marrows are rather greedy but not very particular about their food; they are also thirsty. Plenty of half-rotted compost supplemented with a little animal manure in a similar condition will suit their needs, and if this is buried under 5–7.5 cm (2–3 in) of soil it will also serve as a sponge for retaining moisture. The leading shoots of trailing marrows should be pinched out at quite an early stage as described for cucumbers. Encouraging side branching in this way helps to avoid the annoying habit (pumpkins especially) of concentrating all their energy into one enormous fruit, to such an extent that other fruit which have started to swell promisingly are starved of nourishment and drop off. Preparation 501 is given when the first fruit have set.

All marrows bear male and female flowers separately. Although bumble bees visit both sorts of flower, it is usually advisable to do some hand pollination, especially with pumpkins. The female flowers, distinguished by a bulge beneath the petals, open early in the morning and are 'receptive' for several hours; the pollen is ripe in the males at the same time, so the job must be done before midday. A male flower is picked, the petals stripped off and the pollen bearing centre is placed into the female. It sometimes happens that there are no male flowers on a plant when needed; in this case a male can usually be found on another trailing plant not necessarily of the same variety. Cross-pollinated fruit must not be kept for seed.

Little Gem squash is a less vigorous but very prolific type of trailer and, if it is necessary to conserve space, it can be grown on an upright frame or strong peasticks. The fruits reach the size of tennis balls and are harvested as soon as they stop swelling; they are cooked whole, then cut in half and buttered. Unfortunately seed is not readily obtained in Britain and may have to be brought in from South Africa. Once it has been grown it is possible to save one's own seed for the future, provided that the advice given in Appendix A is followed in detail. Properly stored, the seed will remain viable for at least eight years.

Among the bush types zucchinis and courgettes are the most satisfactory to grow. Two plants are enough to give a regular supply for a small household for six to eight weeks. In a large garden where more plants are grown they will come into the fruit break of the rotation spaced at 90 cm (3 ft) apart; but a couple of plants can usually be fitted into an odd corner or among soft fruit bushes. Both types are generally eaten immature and are cut at the stage when the remains of the flower at the tip of the fruit have completely withered and fall off when touched. If left longer on the plants courgettes form small striped marrows about 23 cm (9 in) long; the dark green zucchinis will grow to 45 cm (18 in). Both are very palatable when cooked as vegetable marrows.

All kinds of marrow are very succulent in the early stages and are therefore attractive to slugs and snails, so it is advisable to take precautions against them.

Sweet Corn

Sweet corn is another rewarding crop which can be taken in the fruit break of the rotation. If given a generous supply of compost it may be planted at 45 cm (18 in) spacing or even closer in the rows instead of the 60 cm (2 ft) recommended in seed catalogues. On the other hand, at a wider spacing of 60 cm by 75 cm (2 ft by 2½ ft) it can be interplanted with french beans—a combination adopted traditionally by many African tribes. The beans, however, will be difficult to harvest regularly, so a variety which can be left to ripen as haricots is to be preferred.

Seed is usually sown in boxes at 5 cm (2 in) apart, or singly in 6 cm (2½ in) pots or soil blocks, towards the end of April under cover for transplanting in June. Sowing can also be done in the open in May; in this case the pots with two seeds each can profitably be covered with wide-mouthed glass jars to give extra warmth and protection against possible late frost. When the stronger seedlings reach the top of the jars, the jars are removed and the weaker seedlings uprooted.

In order to ensure good pollination the crop is grown in blocks, never as a single long row. The pollen is produced in the 'tassels' on the tops of the plants and drifts in the air onto the 'silks' protruding from the embryo cobs lower down. The process can be assisted on a small scale by shaking the tassels in the late morning. 501 is sprayed just before the tassels are ready to emerge and a later spray can be given when the cobs are swelling. Tastes differ as to the best time to harvest; some people like to have a floury grain to chew, while others prefer it to be more succulent. A good general guide is to pick the cobs when the silks are completely withered; but it is always possible to split open part of the covering sheath and 'have a peep'.

Many of the varieties on sale are F¹ hybrids, especially those which have been bred for the more northerly areas, so it is useless to try to save one's own seed even if a cob should ripen sufficiently for the purpose. The plants tend to go on producing small cobs from side shoots, but by then the tassels have shed most of their pollen, so these small late cobs set very little seed unless one or two plants are sown about three weeks after the main crop to act as pollinators.

There are no serious pests or diseases except for slugs and sparrows on young seedlings. Failure to grow a satisfactory crop can be due to poor pollination in wet weather, to insufficient compost, or to a cooler than normal August.

Tomatoes

There can be very few gardeners who do not attempt by some means or other to grow their own tomatoes. It is a moot point whether this is due to the inferior quality of much of the commercial crop, or whether it is the challenge presented by the rather special nature of the tomato plant. In his agriculture lectures Rudolf Steiner described it as 'the most uncompanionable creature in the whole plant kingdom. It does not want to get anything from outside.' In the animal and human organism its independence is matched by that of the liver; hence it is useful for counteracting morbid conditions in that organ. On the other hand its independent nature stimulates the growth of carcinomas and tumours, so anyone threatened with cancer should avoid them.

Tomatoes can be grown in many different situations, perhaps yet another reason for their popularity. Conditions may vary from beds or pots in a heated or cold greenhouse to sunny sheltered spots in the open, with tubs on a verandah as another possibility; so far as is known, nobody has yet devised a biodynamic grow-bag. The description of preliminary cultural operations for a greenhouse bed which follows can be adapted for containers and outdoor planting: this is not a rule of thumb method to be followed in detail, but is given to illustrate the general needs of the plants. Two or three weeks before the young plants are ready to go out a shallow trench not more that 12.5 cm (5 in) deep is dug along the planting line. It is filled with 7.5 cm (3 in) of half-rotted compost and animal manure mixed with wood ashes which are covered over to form a low ridge. Any available comfrey leaves (perhaps dried for the purpose during the previous year) are included with the manure. Preparation 500 is sprayed just before or soon after the operation. The formation of a ridge allows the soil to warm up more easily than in a flat bed and stimulates the working of the cosmic influences. A warm soil is essential if the young plants are not to receive a check after being moved; many early disappointments are caused by a cold soil. It is hard to believe how long it takes a bed to warm up even in a heated greenhouse. In cool conditions it sometimes pays to put bottles into the future planting holes and fill them two or three times with boiling water. A crop of lettuce can be taken if seedlings have been got ready to transplant along the lower sides of the ridge soon after it has been made. A light mulch of leafmould or other fine material is applied to the ridge to prevent the sides from being eroded by watering. As mentioned earlier, it is a good plan to sink 10 cm (4 in) pots along the top of the ridge between the tomato plants; these can then be regularly filled with water to ensure that the deeper roots of the plants are kept well supplied with moisture; tomatoes are all too prone to make most of their roots very close to the surface and this makes them vulnerable to wilting during a hot spell.

Tomato plants can of course be bought in when the time is ripe, but since bio-dynamic growers are likely to be looking for quality as a priority there will probably be difficulty in finding the varieties of their choice. In any case it is more satisfying to raise one's own seedlings and grow them bio-dynamically from the start. There is a great temptation, even without a heated greenhouse, to start too soon and to sow the seed in January or February. March is quite early enough; without heat mid-April onwards is quite satisfactory. It is worth remembering that tomatoes need plenty of light as well as warmth for their best development. Seed is best sown singly in a pan spaced 2.5 cm (1 in) apart; the pan can be put on a boiler or radiator to start the germination which needs a temperature of 15°C (60°F). As soon as the first signs of a true leaf appear the strongest seedlings are selected and transferred to soil blocks or 6 cm (2½ in) pots filled with a rich potting compost. When roots can be seen coming through the bottom of the pots the plants are moved to larger pots where they will remain until going out into the bed. The time taken from sowing to planting out will vary according to light and warmth conditions; a rough average is two-and-a-half months, but late sowings will come on more quickly. When repotting or transplanting tomato seedlings it is a good practice to put them in at least 1 cm (½ in) deeper than before; in this way root growth from the base of the stem is stimulated, and the resulting plants will be sturdier. The best stage for planting out is when the first flower bud can just be discerned. The plants are trained to single stems on strings or canes. All side growths springing from the leaf axils are pinched out regularly; these shoots can be put into a jar of water to make a *jauche* which is later diluted and applied as a foliar spray.

In his agriculture lectures Rudolf Steiner suggested making a special compost from all parts of the tomato plants when they are pulled up, so that the next year's plants may grow and flourish on the remnants of the old. There is never enough of such compost for the full needs of the new crop, and the compost, standing through the winter, is seldom ready in time. Such a compost, however, made with a little manure in the autumn, does provide some useful material for adding to the main bed as an extra mulch when the first trusses are setting fruit. This mulch, together with any available comfrey leaves and stalks, is again covered with leafmould or the remains of the previous mulch so that it is kept moist and active. As explained in an earlier chapter comfrey is rich in the potash which tomatoes need for their best development.

In the mornings the flower trusses are gently tapped or shaken to assist pollination. An alternative, especially during dry weather, is to spray the flowers with water at no lower temperature than the surrounding air. Although tomatoes are reputed to like a dry atmosphere, some humidity round the flowers is essential to prevent the arrested development which sometimes appears as static green pinheads where fruit should be swelling: this condition may also occur in plants which are rather weak through low temperatures or poor development in soil which was too cold at planting time Preparation 501 is first sprayed in the morning when the fruit begins to set, and subsequently whenever a little can be saved from the treatment of other crops.

For growing in the open there are several comparatively new bush varieties. Seedlings are raised in the same way as for greenhouse plants, but they should not be planted out before the beginning of June unless they are protected by cloches; cloches are also useful for ripening off late fruit. Bush plants do not have to be staked or pinched out, but they do need a thick straw mulch to keep the fruit off the ground, away from slugs. The small-fruited delicious 'cherry' varieties are also good for outside growing; they are allowed to branch and are best planted against some kind of trellis for support, but these also can be allowed to sprawl if space permits.

The tomato grower need not worry much about insect troubles except for whiteflies which can be a serious nuisance in a greenhouse; they are not indigenous to Britain but have been introduced unwittingly. Quite recently a predator has also been introduced, this time intentionally, and it is now possible to buy some of these tiny scoliid wasps (*Encarsia formosa*) together with some whiteflies.[1] The two are put onto the crop at an early

1 Obtainable from; English Woodlands Control, Hoyle, Graffham, Petworth, W. Sussex.

stage and soon establish a balance in which there are always some whiteflies but never enough of them to cause harm. This method of biological control is well worth adopting in a larger greenhouse, but there does not seem to be much information as to its cost effectiveness on a small scale. Some success against whitefly has been claimed and proved by planting dwarf or French marigolds (*Tagetes*) among the tomato plants. However, the planting of tomatoes does not automatically imply that whitefly will find them. (See also the advice on nettles as a foliar spray, p. 93.)

Sometimes a plant or two may become infected with virus which may be brought in on the hands of pipe and cigarette smokers. The leaves become so chlorotic, wrinkled and distorted that no worthwhile fruit is produced; any infected plants should be removed as soon as the symptoms are noticed.

Plants in the open (only very rarely those under glass) are susceptible to the same blight which occurs on potatoes: the same precautions are applicable and should be put in hand at once if the disease has been noticed on a nearby potato crop. If only a few plants are involved, the spread of the disease can be delayed by removing and burning any leaves which develop the typical black patches. But once the disease has gained a hold the only course is to strip the plants of any fruit and uproot them.

PERENNIAL CROPS

Globe Artichokes

This is definitely a crop for the epicure and the ordinary mortal need not bother to grow the large flowering heads which some people rave about. Unlike some of the perennial croppers, globe artichokes should not be tucked away in odd corners, nor are they suitable for the main vegetable plot. The ideal place for them is a sunny spot in the ornamental part of the garden where they will produce a mass of silvery-tinted foliage to form a background for other flowers. It takes three years before a plant grown from seed will yeild a flower head worth cooking: the period is reduced to two years if plants are grown from offshoots. Spaced at 90 cm (3 ft) apart they need a rich soil and should be given an annual spring mulch of compost or manure. Preparation 500 is sprayed on the surrounding soil before spring growth starts, and 501 when the first signs of flowering stems can be seen in the hearts at the base of the leaves.

Jerusalem Artichokes

This is an entirely different type of plant from the globe and the two are not even closely related botanically. Jerusalem artichokes, though not a true perennial, are included here because they do not easily fit into the root break of a crop rotation and usually occupy the same ground for several years. The name 'Jerusalem' does not refer to their place of origin which lies in the region of Nova Scotia; it seems to have arisen in the seventeenth century (when they were first introduced into Europe) as a mispronunciation. The plant is a near relation of the sunflower, but only very rarely does it flower on the top of its 210 cm (7 ft) stems, and when they do flower it is too late in the season for any seed to develop. In the tropics it has quite a different habit and grows into a bushy plant not more than 120 cm (4 ft) high which becomes covered in a mass of small sunflowers; but even these do not set viable seed. Propagation is therefore always done by planting tubers.

The tubers of the common type are inclined to be very knobbly, it pays to select smooth tubers about the size of a small egg for planting in February, but even from these sets there will nearly always be some badly shaped tubers at harvest time. Two more recent varieties, Silver Skin and Fuseau, overcome this trouble to a certain extent, but the latter are rather long and thin with a consequently high proportion of skin. Seed tubers are planted about 10 cm (4 in) deep and 45 cm (18 in) apart with 75 cm (30 in) between the rows. Yields of 500 g–1 kg (1–2 lb) per plant can usually be obtained in a good soil without further manuring, but a generous dressing of compost worked in before planting will treble this amount. Tuber formation does not really get under way until mid-August. It is not worth trying to harvest until the leaves are dying back; so long as they remain green they are increasing the crop down below. Some gardening books and articles recommend artichokes as a wind-break, but they do not mention that the tall stems themselves will need strong support against wind; in any case they will only give wind protection during late summer and autumn.

The crop is best left in the ground until required, but if more is lifted the surplus must be stored in moist earth because the tubers dry out very quickly. However carefully one harvests the crop, some tubers will inevitably be left in the ground to come up in the following year. Nevertheless, after digging up a plant for use, it is quite a good plan to replant one suitable tuber and mark the spot with a stick. If given an annual mulch of compost, artichokes can be grown on the same plot for four to five years, but after that it is advisable to move them to another site. In the kitchen it is not necessary to go through the tedious and wasteful task of peeling the tubers—the skins will come off very easily after boiling. A watch must, however, be kept for slug holes: slugs are the crop's worst enemy, and cannot be successfully trapped in the ground. Treatment with Fertosan has proved ineffective more than once, but Maria Thun's remedy has shown some promise.

Rhubarb

Most gardeners like to have a few rhubarb crowns tucked away in an odd corner and there will almost certainly be a rhubarb bed if one moves into a house with an established garden. Such beds will probably be rather old. They may have been starved and it could be difficult to determine the variety. More often than not it will be advisable to start a new bed. As the plants are very deep rooted and will be there for several years, the new bed must be given a sound foundation. Take out a trench at least 60 cm (2 ft) wide and 45 cm (18 in) deep, putting the paler subsoil aside separately; then replace this subsoil with such materials as shoddy, feathers, an old flock mattress, turf (provided that it is free from perennial weeds), bashed bones, old brassica stems and any other tough organic waste which is available locally. Mix in some good bio-dynamic compost and spray 500 with the compost preparations before covering it over with the topsoil firmly trodden in.

Rhubarb can be grown from seed, but it will be three years

before even a small picking can be taken from plants raised in this way. The more usual method of propagation is to plant crowns which may be bought in, cadged from a friend, or taken from old plants of one's own. In the latter case dig up the whole of an old plant in the autumn when the leaves have died back, cut it into large chunks with a spade and leave out in the open exposed to snow and frost. In March cut the chunks up further and select for planting pieces 23–30 cm (9–12 in) long which have a firm root and a strong bud. Pieces with small buds and partly rotten roots are discarded; they will not decompose easily in the compost heap unless they are finely chopped up. The selected crowns are planted vertically 90 cm (3 ft) apart with the buds just showing at the surface. Four mature plants will easily supply the needs of an average family.

In the autumn, when even the largest old leaves have shrivelled away to almost nothing, rhubarb beds are cleaned up and quite a light cultivation is given, taking care to loosen any patches which have become compacted during picking. Then 500 is sprayed and a thin mulch of half-rotted manure or compost is applied; this is then covered with several centimetres of dead leaves anchored with some bracken or old peasticks; if bracken is plentiful, it can be used instead of the leaves. The variety Timperly's Early will push its first shoots through the mulch soon after Christmas. These shoots, though small, are delicious when cooked, and it does not weaken the plant to take them; if they are not used, they will be killed off by the first hard frost. In addition to its earliness and excellent flavour, Timperly Early has the great advantage that it hardly ever wastes its substance by sending up flowering stems; as with other varieties, any flowering stems which do appear must be cut back to the crown as soon as possible.

Seakale

There are two ways of growing seakale which, when blanched, makes a pleasant addition to early spring salads or else is stewed like celery. If grown from 'thongs' or root cuttings it can be treated as an annual in the root break of the rotation. In this case the plants are lifted in the autumn when the top growth has died down; the main roots are stored for forcing while the side roots are used for planting. The latter are cut square at the top end and sloping at the lower so that it will be easy to plant them the right way up; 10–15 cm (4–6 in) is the best length. They can be kept out of doors covered in a sheltered place, or in a cellar, until planting time in March. The other way is to treat like rhubarb, several crowns being established from thongs spaced at 60–90 cm (2–3 ft) apart in a fairly open corner. These are blanched *in situ* by covering in February with large pots or boxes from which all light must be excluded, or else by covering with leaves to a depth of 23–30 cm (9–12 in). It is inadvisable to blanch in the first year after planting unless very strong growth has been made. The blanched shoots are cut at ground level and the crowns will then shoot again to store nourishment for the following year. A bed of this kind will crop for about four years before dying out. Roots stored for forcing are kept cool and slightly moist until required. Forcing is accomplished by putting three or four roots into a large pot or similar container and packing them in with moist peat or old potting soil. The pots must then be covered to ensure complete darkness and allow at last 23 cm (9 in) clearance for the shoots; black polythene bags are not very suitable because they exclude air. A minimum temperature of 15°C (60°F) is necessary.

Seakale likes a rich soil, and if the second method of growing is adopted the bed is prepared in the same way as for rhubarb. Thongs are not always readily obtainable, so it may be necessary to grow from seed which is sown in April and thinned to 30 cm (1 ft) apart. Growth is slower than from thongs and it is normally advisable to leave the plants in the ground for a second year of growth before taking them up for forcing, but one year's growth is quite enough for thong production.

QUALITY

So far very little has been said about that somewhat nebulous term 'quality', the attainment of which in our vegetables and fruit is one of the main aims of bio-dynamic practice. Modern research effort has been so focused on obtaining maximum yields that the more subtle aspects of plant and animal products, which are very difficult to analyse and weigh, have been over-shadowed. True, keeping quality is recognised, but the main conventional criterion of quality is immaculate appearance. Nutritive quality is judged purely on chemical composition—types and amounts of protein, carbohydrates, fats, vitamins and so on. Appeals to the senses of taste and smell are seldom considered.

What, then, are the bio-dynamic criteria of quality? How are they attained, and how are they judged? Implicit in all that has been described earlier and in all that stems from Rudolf Steiner's agriculture lectures is the notion that the plant kingdom springing upwards from the earth must, for its fullest development, be permeated through and through not only with what can be derived from a living soil but also with influences streaming in from the universe. Ripening processes are just as important as growth processes. When nourished by such plants men and animals are brought into tune with the cosmos as a whole; not only is man's physical body harmonised but his activities of thinking, feeling and willing are also rightly stimulated. Appearance is an ancillary factor, by no means unimportant, but aroma and flavour come into play as well and help to activate the digestive processes in a beneficial way. From another point of view one could say that, when bio-dynamically treated, the life forces of the plants are brought to the peak of perfection, and this factor is transmitted to the consumer. Balance and harmony are created.

Although some physical and chemical tests for this kind of quality have been devised, its extent is largely gauged by two methods—sensitive crystallisation and chromatography. Both these methods in one way or another vividly portray in pictorial form harmony and the living strength (or lack of them) in the products under test. By such means also it has been shown that the quality depends to quite a large extent on seasonal influences. In a dull and wet summer quality is not so high as in a bright and sunny one. But when produce grown under various systems—straight organic, conventional and bio-dynamic—is tested, the bio-dynamic products almost invariably come out on top. In a poor year the bio-dynamic quality may be as low as that attained by the use of artificial fertilisers in a good year.

CHAPTER 17
Herbs

No garden is really complete without its culinary and other herbs, not only for the benefit of the housewife, but also for the more subtle healing influences which they have on their surroundings. It is convenient to set aside a sunny patch for the perennial culinaries such as lovage, thyme, sage and so on. They do not need a rich soil; in fact their aroma is impaired if they are encouraged to make lush growth. A light annual dressing of fully mature compost with an autumn spray of 500 and 501 in the spring is all that they require. Parsley can be grown as a border rotated round the vegetable garden. Contrary to accepted practice, fine results can be obtained by sowing parsley in a deep pan with some extra warmth in the spring and transplanting the seedlings singly at about 10 cm (4 in) apart when they have made two or three main leaves. Occasionally parsley plants will cease to thrive and their leaves will turn a mauve colour; this is often due to attack by carrot root fly and the only remedy is to eradicate them and start again.

The virtues of some herbs are often extolled as repellants against insect nuisances on vegetable crops. Although there is undoubtedly an element of truth in such claims, they cannot be relied upon to operate under all conditions. Perhaps the implicit faith of the gardener in their effectiveness is the main factor for success. Nevertheless it seems certain that a few herbal plants round the vegetable garden, also among fruit trees and bushes, do have a beneficial effect; but as these effects are often of a qualitative nature it is almost impossible to prove them scientifically. Among these herbs there can be included some of the plants used for making the compost preparations—yarrow, chamomile and valerian. In a large garden there may even be a place for a clump of nettles which regulate the working of iron in their surroundings and whose young shoots in the spring make such excellent soup. In this connection it is perhaps worth quoting what Rudolf Steiner has to say about yarrow in *Agriculture*: 'Yarrow is always the greatest boon . . . like sympathetic people in human society who have a favourable influence by their mere presence and not by anything they say.' Again, a plant of wormwood is useful in the spring to signal the arrival of any blackfly, for they like this plant even better than broad beans; it is an early warning which may stimulate predators or which may indicate that precautionary measures, if not already taken, must be put in hand at once.

Herbs in the Vegetable Garden (*by K. Castelliz*)

In the years after the Second World War it was very difficult to grow herbs, except for the most common ones like parsley, sage and one or two more, because one could not get the seeds. Today it is quite difficult to imagine such a state of affairs. There is a widespread interest in herbs, and many people drink herb teas either for pleasure or for reasons of health.

What is it that makes a herb into what it is? What is the difference between a vegetable and a herb?

Our vegetables are fascinating enough. They are highly specialised plants, designed for human consumption. We have root vegetables like carrots and parsnips, stem vegetables such as beetroot, turnip and kohl rabi—in all three of these we eat the expanded stem—leaf vegetables like cabbage, spinach and lettuce. Cauliflower is an inflorescence and in sweet corn we eat the seed.

We can say that through the breeding of food plants from wild plants, the part which we actually eat—be it raw or cooked— has taken on the character of fruit. The carrot, for instance, is a fruit in the region of the root. It has taken on a bright colour, is sweet and has developed an unrootlike aroma. The cabbage is a fruit in the leaf region and has achieved this by packing its leaves so tightly that it has become a ball. Kohl rabi and beetroot are swollen stems, stem-fruits. Cauliflower is a fruit in the realm of the flower.

When we enter a vegetable garden during the growing season, everything we see is green and leafy, with the exception of peas and beans, unless we have also planted flowers. Without these the garden is lacking in flowers and their scent to balance the leafy element. This is where the herbs come in.

Most of our herbs develop their flowering *impulse* before they actually flower. A rose has its heavenly scent in the flower. It gives it away freely before it withers and forms seeds.

Not so our herbs. They do not wait for a scented flower to appear, but their flowering process has slipped down into the region of the leaf where it is manifest as soon as the leaves develop, and it is this displacement that makes herbs so potent, either for culinary or medicinal use.

If herbs grow in the vegetable garden, the vegetables actually benefit from their scent—that is, from their particular flowering process. Annual herbs like dill or summer savory can find their place at the end of a bed. Larger ones or perennial herbs can be planted anywhere or can have a bed or border to themselves.

A bio-dynamic herb garden. *Photo: J. Anderson*

More about Herbs (*by B. Saunders-Davies*)

ANGELICA (*Angelica archangelica*)
The native *Angelica sylvestris* is a handsome, almost architectural plant with its smooth purple stems, large umbels of almost white flowers and large, elegant leaves, but for culinary purposes *A. archangelica* is used. It is a native of northern Europe, especially Iceland and Lapland. Buy plants. If cut in May the tender stalks can be eaten raw. They are sweet but slightly bitter. They can be added to rhubarb jam in the proportion of 1 to 4. Angelica is chiefly used for candying and should be cut in May and June. An old recipe advises: Cut into 3-inch (7-cm) lengths, boil in very little water, peel and boil again until green. Dry with a cloth. Put to stand for two days with an equal quantity of sugar by weight. Boil again until clear and green. Sprinkle with as much castor sugar as will adhere to it. Let it dry in a very slow oven but do not let it get hard.

BALM (see Lemon Balm)

BASIL (*Ocimum basilicum*)
Sweet basil is very tender and will not stand any frost. It is best sown from March to early May under cover and transplanted. It makes a bushy plant about 45 cms (18 ins) high. It goes particularly well with tomatoes, egg dishes and lamb, and can be used in soups and casseroles. A pinch of it, finely chopped, will add a new flavour to a salad. Leaves can be picked while the plant is growing but the main crop for drying should be cut just as the flower buds are ready to open. The plants will probably sprout again and a few can be brought into the house or conservatory to provide fresh leaves for the winter. If kept on a windowsill it keeps flies away.

Bush basil (*Ocimum minimum*) can be grown as a pot plant for its fragrance.

BORAGE (*Borago officinalis*)
Germination is sometimes difficult but once established it seeds itself. Sow in April, transplant while very young and with great care as it does not like being moved. The young leaves have a

flavour somewhat like cucumber and can be used, finely shredded, in green salads and cottage cheese. The glorious blue flowers are beautiful in the garden and make delightful decoration for many dessert dishes. Bees love it.

CARAWAY (*Carum carvi*)
This is a biennial. The seeds are often added to red cabbage, rye bread and some cakes. The root can be boiled as a vegetable and has a spicy taste.

CHAMOMILE
Two species of the chamomile family are used as herbs. *Anthemis nobilis* is a perennial of prostrate habit much used in the old days for aromatic lawns and requiring frequent mowing and rolling. *Matricaria recutita* (formerly known as *Matricaria chamomilla* or *Chamomilla officinalis*) is an annual, often called German or Wild Chamomile, and is the one used to make the bio-dynamic compost preparation. The dried flowers of both species can be used as a tea to aid digestion or as a soothing drink in the evening. Once established, the annual sows itself.

CHERVIL (*Anthriscus cerefolium*)
The seed does not retain its viability for long, but once established will sow itself. It can be used like parsley and is excellent in an omelette and in a mixed salad. The root can be boiled and eaten as a salad.

CHIVES (*Allium schoenoprasum*)
These are the most delicately flavoured of the onion tribe. The easiest way to propagate is to take a few bulbs from old clumps and plant out in good soil, or buy a pot of seedlings. They soon multiply and the clumps should be divided occasionally. They grow all through the summer and are invaluable for salads, omelettes, in cottage cheese and cheese dips and with tomatoes and soups. Their mauve flowers are attractive in a vase with some fine silver foliage such as santolina.

CORIANDER (*Coriandrum sativum*)
This native of Southern Europe, Egypt and the East grows to

about 90 cm (3 ft) high. The seeds improve in flavour the longer they are kept. The leaves can be used in salads and the seeds in curry, chutney and cream cheese.

DILL (*Anethum graveolens*)

An annual, dill does not like an acid soil, so add a little lime. Sow thinly, in trays preferably, and plant out in little clumps. It is particularly good with fish, cucumber salad and potatoes. It is used when pickling cucumber and gherkins and can be added to other pickles, soups and stews.

FENNEL (*Foeniculum vulgare* and *F. dulce*)

Our tall native wild fennel is a most elegant and decorative plant. The fine leaves, fresh or dried, go well with fish. Like parsley, they can be used as a sauce or chopped fine in melted butter. The Florence fennel (*F. dulce*) is a popular vegetable on the continent (see Chapter 16).

GARLIC (*Allium sativum*)

There are many cloves in each bulb and they should be planted about 5 cm (2 in) deep and 15 cm (6 in) apart from November to February and harvested from July to late summer.

For wild garlic see Ransoms.

HYSSOP (*Hyssopus officinalis*)

This shrubby plant can be raised from seed or cuttings. It can be planted in the autumn but needs a little winter protection. The leaves are quite pungent and for drying should be gathered before flowering. The typical flower is a glorious blue, although there are pink and white varieties. Bees love it. It can be trimmed as a low hedge but that sacrifices the flowers.

LAVENDER

There are many species but the two most usual are *Lavendula spica* with its many varieties and *L. vera* which yields the best oil of lavender and lavender water. It is more likely to be planted in the flower garden than the herb garden, as it associates so well with many plants, is evergreen and spreads it delightful scent widely. It is easily increased by cuttings taken in early spring or

October. For drying, the flower spikes should be cut in the early morning for best aroma, and dried indoors out of the sun. To keep the bushes tidy, they should be pruned after cutting the flowers. For fascinating lavender lore, read Eleanor Sinclair Rhodes' *Herbs and Herb Gardening*.

LEMON BALM (*Melissa officinalis*)
This hardy perennial can be propagated from seed, cuttings or by division. Its lemon flavour can be utilised in many ways, as a herb tea, chopped up fine in salads, to add to a sauce or to scent a bath.

LOVAGE (*Ligusticum levisticum*)
This is a large and decorative plant, often growing to over 120 cm (4 ft). It likes a fairly heavy soil and lasts for many years. It is a spicy herb and can be used in all sorts of meat and vegetable dishes, soups and sauces. One leaf, finely chopped, adds an unusual flavour to a salad. It can be propagated by seed or root division in spring or autumn.

MARIGOLD (*Calendula officinalis*)
These come in many varieties both single and double and in shades of colour varying from pale yellow to the deepest orange. The petals are very decorative in salads and the dried petals were much used in the sixteenth to eighteenth centuries in broths, also to impart a golden colour to foods and to deepen the colour of fair hair. They are cut down by frost but usually seed themselves, though it is wiser to gather some seed for the following year.

The French marigold (*Tagetes patula*) also has charming flowers and both the roots and the leaves have such a strong odour that they are inimical to some root pests and to whitefly. Plant among tomatoes and other crops.

MARJORAM (*Origanum vulgare*)
This is our native species and is at home on the chalk downs. The flowers are delightfully scented and rich in nectar for the bees. It is a hardy perennial. There are many other varieties, mostly from the Mediterranean and therefore tender and better treated

as annuals. They are even more aromatic and more used for culinary purposes. There is Sweet Marjoram (*O. marjorana*), Pot Marjoram (*O. onites*), Winter Marjoram (*O. herodioticum*), hardy in sheltered positions, and many others. It is easier to buy young plants as the seeds are very small and the seedlings delicate to handle. All the marjorams are good in egg dishes and sausages and with all kinds of meat and poultry. They have a stimulating flavour and aid digestion.

MINTS

There are so many species with different flavours that only a few will be mentioned. The one usually used for mint sauce is the spearmint (*Mentha viridis*), but why not try apple mint (*M. rotundifolia*), a beautiful plant with spikes of mauve flowers and greyish woolly leaves growing to 120 or 150 cm (4 or 5 ft). It has a much more delicate flavour and dries well. Crush some and sprinkle over lamb chops or add it to any mixture of herbs in cottage cheese. Add a few leaves to peas. It makes a very pleasant herb tea. There is also peppermint (*M. piperita*) for herb tea, and many others. Beware where you plant mints: they spread in an uncontrollable manner and should be restricted in some way. Propagate by dividing.

MUGWORT (see Wormwood)

NASTURTIUM (*Tropaeolum majus*)

Both climbing and dwarf varieties are available. The flowers and the peppery leaves can be added to salads and the seeds, when green, can be pickled like capers. Planted among vegetables it can attract blackfly away from other crops. Planted around apple trees it can be a deterrent to woolly aphis (American blight).

PARSLEY (*Carum petroselenum*)

Most people only know the curled parsley, but if you can get the smooth-leaved variety it is much more aromatic. There is also a root parsley, Hamburg parsley, obtainable from some seedsmen. It has an excellent flavour in soup, rather like celery. Parsley can be sown in trays or in the open in March or April on a fine tilth, well firmed and watered. The root variety should be treated like carrots and the thinnings chopped up for casseroles or soup. It is advisable to mark the rows with a few radishes, as parsley is slow to germinate. It is an indispensable herb, raw or cooked in rissoles, sauces, salads, soups and casseroles, and is very helpful for digesting heavy foods such as potatoes. It stimulates the kidneys and the whole process of digestion. It is rich in iron and vitamin A.

It usually overwinters and a few strong plants can be left to produce seed. A few plants can be potted up and brought indoors to supply fresh leaves during the winter. It dries well and can also be frozen in bunches. For seed, the stems should be cut as soon as the umbels are dark brown. These should be dried in an airy place, under cover.

RANSOMS or WILD GARLIC (*Allium ursinum*)

It is not generally known that the young leaves, boiled, make a delicious spinach. Obtain plants from wildflower specialists but beware, it can be very invasive! The attractive white flowers last well as cut flowers. If you notice a slight garlic smell, change the water after half an hour. Some other wild plants that make good spinach are: Good King Henry (*Chenopodium Bonus Henricus*), Fat Hen (*Chenopodium album*) and Orach (*Atriplex hortensis*). The variety *A. hortensis rubra* is very ornamental.

ROSEMARY (*Rosmarinus officinalis*)

Many beautiful legends are attached to rosemary. It was considered a holy herb with power against evil, the devil and witches. It is a native of the Mediterranean and cannot stand very severe frost, but in a sunny, sheltered spot its little blue flowers are a joy throughout the winter, reaching their climax in June. It is much appreciated by bees. It can make a large bush and can even be trained to cover a wall. It is easily propagated from cuttings. It adds a Provençal flavour to lamb and other meat dishes. A sprig added to cabbage or casseroles is good.

RUE (*Ruta graveolens*)

A native of Southern Europe, it has a long history of anti-plague, anti-magical and medicinal properties. Its unusual blue-green foliage is attractive and lasts through the winter but needs a sheltered position. It can be propagated either from seed sown in spring or by cuttings taken in late spring.

SAGE (*Salvia officinalis*)

Sage, with its greyish green or purplish leaves and spikes of usually bluish-purple flowers, is an attractive shrubby herb, held in high esteem in earlier times. The leaves, fresh or dried, make a valuable tea for the relief of sore throat or to check the beginning of a cold. It can also be chewed. In sage and onion stuffing it goes well with pork, veal, rabbit, goose, turkey and chicken. Propagation by cuttings is easy.

Santolina chamaecyparis

A most decorative medicinal herb with bright silver foliage and round yellow flower heads on longish stalks. It can grow into a low bush. Both foliage and flowers mix well in small flower arrangements. Cuttings strike easily.

SAVORY

The annual summer savory (*Satureia hortensis*) and the perennial winter savory (*S. montana*) both have quite a strong aromatic flavour and are used more on the Continent than in Britain. The herb is especially good added to beans—in fact in Germany it is called *Bohnenkraut*, 'bean herb'. It can also be used as seasoning for lentil soup, peas and tomatoes. The very fine seeds of summer savory can be sown in March or April and later transplanted or thinned to about 15 cm (6 in) apart. Likewise winter savory, but being a perennial it can also be propagated by cuttings. It has a rather stronger flavour than the summer species. To dry, cut the shoots just before flowering.

SORREL

Our native wild species, *Rumex acetosa*, is very acid as its name implies and must be used sparingly, but the broad-leaved cultivated varieties of the continental *R. scutatus* are better for making sorrel soup and sharpening sauces. Sorrel combines well with mint, parsley and onions. A very little can be shredded into a salad. Grow from seed, but the French species will last for about three years if prevented from flowering.

SOUTHERNWOOD or 'OLD MAN' (see Wormwood)

SWEET CICELY (*Myrrhis odorata*)
This makes a charming feathery-leaved bushy plant, eventually reaching 120 cm (4 ft) or more. The leaves, chopped, add a subtle flavour to salads, and the long seeds, while green, are spicy and good in salads dressed with oil and vinegar. They aid the digestive processes. The delicate white umbels are attractive, and as the plant comes from cool northern climes it will flourish in a shady border and sow itself.

TANSY (*Tanacetum vulgare*)
This bitter, pungent herb should only be used very sparingly if a special tang is required among other flavourings. Its yellow flowers deserve a place in the garden.

TARRAGON (*Artemisia dracunculus* var. sativa)
The true French tarragon seldom flowers or sets seed and must be propagated from cuttings or division. Seed offered for sale is usually an inferior Siberian variety. Tarragon is tolerant of some shade. In time the plants get quite large. For drying, it must be cut well before flowering as otherwise it loses much of its fragrance. It is good as a salad herb and goes particularly well with chicken, fish and some sauces. It is an ingredient of pickled cucumber and gherkins. Tarragon vinegar should be made with the best white wine vinegar, steeping the leaves for a fortnight. It should be used for sauce tartare.

THYME (*Thymus vulgaris* and many other species)
An indispensable herb that brightens almost any meat or cheese dish and is a member of the basic French *bouquet garni* of bay leaf, thyme and parsley. Sprinkle a little on lamb chops under the grill, or add a little to a herb mixture in cottage cheese. It is a paradise for bees. Even added to the bath it is refreshing. Thyme likes a sandy soil and sun. It is fairly hardy but may not survive a hard winter. It can be propagated by cuttings or

division of old plants in spring or autumn or by seed sown in March or April. For the home gardener, however, it is simpler to buy seedling plants.

WORMWOOD (*Artemisia absinthium*)
A very bitter herb but an elegant silver-leaved plant. Its wild relative, mugwort (*A. vulgaris*), is also a shapely plant and less bitter. It used to be made into a spring tonic. Another relative, southernwood (*A. abrotanum*), sometimes known as 'Old Man', is a delightfully fragrant plant and makes an attractive silvery bush or even a hedge. It needs to be hard-pruned every spring or it gets lanky. Cuttings strike very easily. It looks well with pink or blue flower arrangements. A leaf or two, finely chopped, can be added to toasted cheese or other cheese dishes.

All the wormwoods used to be used as strewing herbs and to keep moths out of clothes and furs.

CHAPTER 18

Special Features of the Garden

Colour is an important feature in the development of a garden's individuality, for in the varied colours of flowers, foliage, fruits and even stems the plant kingdom expresses itself in all its fullness, and thereby brings joy not only to the hearts of men but also to the great being of earth itself. On a well balanced farm colours through the seasons follow Nature's pattern, but a garden has to be planned. In the wild the spring is mainly graced by paler tints of yellow and light blue; these give way to brighter, more pronounced hues, and reds come into the picture as St John's tide approaches. Then in late summer the deeper tints of crimson, brown, purple and gold begin to prevail. A streak of white runs through the whole range—snowdrops, cowparsley, elder and bindweed among others. There are of course many exceptions to this general pattern, but if one bears it in mind when planning and can achieve the sequence to some degree, it will go a long way towards establishing a mood of participation in the rhythm of the year.

The colour display is achieved by means of flowering annuals and shrubs (including roses) but especially through the herbaceous border. Every garden needs these perennials on a scale proportionate to its size. When starting a herbaceous border it is essential to make sure that every trace of perennial weeds such as couch grass, ground elder, bindweed and others is removed; all brought in planting material must also be carefully examined with this end view. The best planting time is November so that the plants will settle down and establish good root systems before new growth starts in the following spring. Ideally the main cleaning operations will be done during early summer when any odd pieces of perennial weeds overlooked during the first digging will soon show themselves. Then sow a quick growing green manure crop after spraying 500, giving a little compost if the soil is at all worn out. The green crop is dug in during the latter half of September, but first apply another spray of 500, this time with the compost preparations stirred in as well to help the green material to decompose. Add as much compost or manure as can be spared and supplement it with two single handfuls each of hoof and bone meal per square metre. This preparatory period provides an opportunity to make a plan showing the positions of the species to be planted, and these are marked with pegs when the ground is ready. Subsequent treatment comprises an annual spray of 500 and a light dressing of compost when cleaning up in late autumn. 501 cannot usefully be applied owing to the different stages of development of the various species.

Lawns

Some kind of lawn, its size depending upon that of the whole area, is a necessary feature of every well-balanced garden; not only is it a place where one can relax from time to time but it also serves as a focus round which other facets of the garden can be arranged. Some gardeners will take great pride and trouble in creating and maintaining a perfect grass sward; others are content with a patch of green which is kept smooth and tidy merely by mowing when it becomes unkempt.

When starting a lawn in a new garden it is sometimes possible to establish it from existing meadow land provided that there are not too many weeds present. Some hard initial work with a dibber, light rolling and frequent cutting with a machine set fairly high will quite soon produce an acceptable result. Establishment from bought-in turf is extremely expensive nowadays and is only justified if very quick results are required; even so turf quality can vary greatly and one may get landed with trouble on this score. Direct sowing is often the simplest and most successful method in the long run. By far the best time to sow is

August-September. Right soil conditions—not too wet and not too dry—are important and probably outweigh the desirability of choosing a time when the moon is in a leaf constellation; with luck the two will coincide. It is, however, necessary to begin preparing the site at least two months in advance so that as many weeds as possible can be eliminated. At this stage, if conditions are right, it would be as well to bear in mind Maria Thun's experience with weeds; she advises cultivating when the moon is in the Lion if one wants a lot of dormant weed seeds to germinate, and to kill off the seedlings by hoeing with the moon in the Goat. The soil must first be worked, by hand or rotavator, to a depth of about 7.5 cm (3 in), stones and perennial weed roots being removed. During the preparation of the fine tilth for the seed bed, 500 is sprayed; some sifted well matured compost with hoof and horn is worked in, the amount depending on the fertility status of the soil. A satisfactory seed rate is 25 g (1 oz) per square metre (yard), but this may be doubled for quicker results if expense is no object. To get an even distribution, half the seed is first spread in one direction and then the other half at right angles to the first. The seed must be firmed in, either with a light wooden roller or by just covering with sifted topsoil. Some form of protection against birds is usually necessary. The first cut is given when the grasses are about 5 cm (2 in) high; it must be done with sharp blades to avoid pulling up the seedlings, which can easily happen if the cutting edges are dull.

Once established, an ordinary lawn does not require a great deal of attention apart from mowing and spraying with 500 once or twice a year when other parts of the garden are being treated: occasional weeding may be necessary to improve its appearance. On the heavier types of soil, however, compaction may give rise to poor growth in time. Various kinds of spiked rollers, some more effective than others, are available for aerating the turf; but by far the best tool, if it can be found, is a hollow-tined fork which brings up thin cylinders of the turf; the holes are then filled by brushing in a mixture of three parts sand to one part of sifted compost supplemented with a little bonemeal.

The Boundary

Every individuality has some kind of containing skin which marks it off from its surroundings and gives an indication of its character: a garden is no exception. Some fortunate people may inherit a high wall facing south or west, ideal for fan-trained fruit trees, perhaps interspersed with a few ornamentals. Others may have a wooden paling, usually about 150 cm (5 ft) high, along one or two sides; these are useful sites for soft fruit such as loganberries, blackberries or fan-trained or cordon goose-berries and red currants. A paling can also form a good background to a herbaceous border. Most gardens, however, are bounded by hedges, and these are generally inherited, leaving us no scope for choice of varieties. Old-established hedges can present problems, for they may harbour brambles, ground elder, bindweed (*Calystegia sepium*) and other perennials which either disfigure the hedge and inhibit the growth of the main species or else spread out into an adjoining part of the garden. It takes a determined effort to eliminate bindweed, but it can be done. Throughout the growing season all young shoots are pulled up at weekly intervals, and after two years the hedge should be practically clear, provided one has a co-operative neighbour. It is not possible to treat ground elder in this way, nor can it be killed out by smothering as may be done in the open. In one known case it has not responded to 'pepper', made from seeds and young shoots, and it was not in any way thwarted by planting *Tagetes patula* as is claimed in some quarters. So one may have to resort to a hormone weedkiller; but another solution is to contain it by burying a row of old roofing slates along the infested part; even so some stolons will find their way through the overlaps, but these are easily removed when the first shoots appear above the ground.

With a new garden it will possibly be necessary to plant one or more hedges, and it is essential to do this job thoroughly. The ground should be well worked over to a width of 90 cm (3 ft) a month or two before planting. For planting, preferably done in late autumn, it is better to take out a trench rather than digging holes so that there is ample room to spread out the roots. The treatment is the same as described for establishing a new row of raspberries. The choice of suitable species to plant in a hedge is very wide, and there is something to be said for a mixture which will give added variety to the background. An example would be holly and hawthorn with an occasional privet among them. On the north and east sides evergreen species will make a thicker protection against cold winds and frosty air in winter and spring. But beware of the various Cupressus species which are so freely advertised; they are difficult to manage and can all too easily get out of control, besides taking an undue share of water and fertility from adjoining beds. On soils which are not too heavy beech will quite quickly form a hedge which is attractive and comparatively easy to look after; on a clay soil it could be replaced by hornbeam.

CHAPTER 19

Suggestions for
Experiment and Observation

In this chapter some observations and preliminary experiments
are described; they have not been fully confirmed, but they offer
useful possibilities if they prove to be correct over a wider range
of conditions and over several seasons.

Cabbage White Butterflies

In 1980 caterpillars of the Large White butterfly were collected;
these are the bigger speckled creatures which feed on the outer
leaves and seldom go down into brassica hearts. They were put
into water in a large jam jar and were left to rot in the
greenhouse until July 1981 when the new brassicas had become
established; the jar needed topping up with more rain water
from time to time. Some of the resulting liquid was then strained
and diluted at about one part to twenty; after stirring vigorously
for ten minutes the solution was sprayed as a fine mist over the
whole brassica block. Although the crop was attacked by Small
White caterpillars, only very few specimens of the Large White
appeared. Yet in another part of the garden there were swarms
of them on swedes and black radish, providing plenty of material for a repeat in 1982. In preparation for 1982 the smaller
bright green caterpillars of the Small White were collected in a
separate pot; they are rather more difficult to get at because they
prefer the hearts and growing points to the outer leaves.

Cabbage Aphid

More extensive and confirmatory work needs to be done on this unpleasant nuisance. Some unco-ordinated observations suggest that these aphids are particularly sensitive to the composition of the plant sap. If the winged adults do not find it to their liking, they will not settle down to form colonies, and sometimes colonies will just disappear, perhaps because the sugar content of the sap has changed. Both nettle *jauche* and seaweed (Maxicrop) have on occasions produced the latter effect, and it would seem worth trying them as preventatives in a garden where the nuisance has occurred in the past. There is, however, a difficulty in applying them as foliar sprays because brassica leaves are very shiny and the spray just runs off the leaves; a little soft soap added to the solution would make it stick, but perhaps soil applications would be more effective. Another possibility is to make a *jauche* or a pepper out of the aphids themselves, but there are several snags to be overcome. First, there would have to be quite a serious infestation before one could get enough of the insect to make either. In making a *jauche* they would have to be ground up into a paste in a mortar in order to break down their waxy coats, and by the time the *jauche* had matured it would be very late in the season; it could of course be kept for the following year. A 'pepper' also is unlikely to be of any value in the season in which it is made.

Carrot Fly

Although some protection has been achieved by mulching the future carrot bed with chopped nettles during the previous autumn and winter, this method is not effective in a 'bad' year. Perhaps, in districts where the fly is prevalent, the only way to obtain a clean crop in all seasons is to deter the fly with a *jauche* or 'pepper'. The difficulty here is that the flies are small and insignificant and are therefore almost impossible to collect for rotting or burning. The larvae also are difficult to extract from infected roots, even in a damaged condition. The most practical way of collection is probably to put damaged roots or pieces of root into a large stoppered jar with some sifted soil or sand. When they are fully grown the larvae leave the root to pupate in the soil. Some adults will emerge and die, but if done late in season most of the pupae will wait for the next spring; it is then quite easy during the early part of the winter to sort out the shiny bright brown creatures and mash them up to rot in water. This method is better than allowing the flies to hatch out for burning when the sun and moon are in the Bull at the end of May or early June as it is rather essential to apply a deterrent spray before this date.

Club Root

In addition to the long rest method of eliminating this disease it has been claimed that a compost made with the diseased and swollen roots and then applied to infected land will do the job more effectively and rapidly. The principle behind this idea is that predatory micro-organisms will proliferate in the compost and will then seek out the dormant fungus spores when the compost is applied to the soil. A difficulty here for the small gardener is that there is unlikely to be enough diseased material to make a satisfactory compost, but a very confident and competent compost maker might include such material in a main heap. Homoeopathic treatment is another possibility. What is known as a 'nosode' is made by potentising diseased material up to the sixth decimal potency (D6 or 6X). This can be done professionally for a small charge. Ten drops of the nosode are stirred for two minutes into 4.5 litres (1 gal) of water, and infected land is sprayed just before a brassica crop is planted. An infected cold frame has been cleared in this way, but the nosode has not yet given complete protection on a larger plot. It would seem that the soil must be thoroughly moist at the time of spraying and that a liberal application is necessary—say 4.5 litres (1 gal) to 4 sq. metres (5 sq. yards).

Jerusalem Artichokes

One difficulty with this crop is that the stems are inclined to be very tall and are therefore liable to be knocked over or broken by strong winds. So it might be worth pinching out the growing points at various heights to encourage a more bushy plant to develop. It would also be necessary to judge to what extent the yield might be affected by this practice.

Potato Eelworm

If one has been unfortunate enough to inherit a garden infected with this eelworm, it might be worth saving all the roots of affected plants and keeping them, after drying, in a sealed container until the following year when they can be burnt at the appropriate time in May or June. It would be advisable to keep part of the ash for a second application a year later. It has also been found by the Henry Doubleday Research Association that root secretions from the plant *Tagetes patula*, grown on infected land, will cause the eelworms to emerge from their dormant cysts; finding no potatoes on which to feed, they perish.

500 and 501

In a small garden, or even when working up to ¼ acre, it is rather out of proportion to spend a whole hour stirring these preparations for use at just the time when they would be most effective, and it is questionable whether this is really necessary. With 500 one can to a certain extent compromise with a spring and autumn spray over the whole area; but this is not an ideal solution to the problem and there are occasions when it seems advisable to treat quite a small plot in order to obtain optimum effects. These remarks apply with even greater force in the case of 501. It therefore appears eminently desirable to devise means of activating small quantities of these preparations quite rapidly. A difficulty here is that there are no easy ways of testing whether and when full activation has been achieved, and it seems that one has to rely largely on intuition, feeling and enthusiasm. In any case a rather larger proportion of preparation to water is needed than that recommended for field use. For instance one unit of 500 (18g or ¾ oz) is sufficient for ⅓ acre in the field, but in the small garden 418 sq. metres (500 sq. yards) might be taken as a rough guide.

Some people have devised their own methods. One consists of shaking small quantities rhythmically in a partly filled bottle for two-and-a-half minutes, as is sometimes done when making homoeopathic remedies (succussion). Another way is to shake a bottle with a circular swirling motion until a vortex is formed; a chaos is then created by inverting the bottle, and the swirl is done in the opposite direction with the bottle upside down: the process is repeated rhythmically for four or five minutes. Yet another idea, seeing that astral forces are involved, invokes the number seven. The required volume is either stirred in a bucket or swirled in a bottle as just described. The operation is carried out in seven stages with a pause between each, and each stage consists of seven stirs or swirls, making 49 in all.

Slugs

Maria Thun's suggestion for controlling slugs was mentioned in Chapter 13, but although some gardeners in this country may have tried it, there are no reports of success or failure; any well-grounded experience would be greatly welcomed for publication. The treatment is not an easy one to perform during the busy time of the year. The Crab is a small constellation and the moon moves through it rather quickly; so it is essential to mark the dates very prominently in one's diary. Preoccupation with other Crab operations may land one up in the Lion and the best time will be missed. Moreover, just when one wants slugs they are often hard to find, but a few old boards or pieces of damped black polythene placed on the ground in likely spots will usually collect a few. It is interesting to note that in an experiment at Rothampstead some years ago regular daily trapping in a garden over an appreciable period failed to bring about any reduction in the daily count. So it would seem that Maria Thun's method, or something similar to it which creates an unfriendly atmosphere to the slugs, is well worth trying wherever they are a serious menace. Alternatively it is possible to keep them down if one can persuade a hedgehog or a couple of toads to take up residence.

Waterglass

Although waterglass cannot be said to 'come within the sphere of life', it is one of the more soluble compounds of silicon and can to a certain extent be enlivened by stirring in water; in fact it has to be stirred for at least five minutes to get it fully dissolved. Its use was described as a possible preventative against gooseberry mildew. This use of it through the soil could well be extended to prevent other fungus attacks, and another case has recently come to light. For two or three years some twelve-year-old pear cordons had suffered from pear rust, a rare disease in this country; many young leaves before becoming fully grown curled up with dark red spots and blotches on the upper surfaces and did not develop. In 1982 two soil applications were given, the first in February when the buds were just starting to swell and the second when they were bursting; rusted leaves were negligible compared with previous years. About 37 g (1½ oz) were well stirred into a gallon of rainwater, and the solution was evenly distributed into five holes along each side of the three cordons. The possibility of trying soil applications of waterglass to alleviate apple scab has already been mentioned, and there are indications that botrytis (grey mould) in strawberries might be prevented or at least greatly reduced in this way. It would also be well worth trying this method against peach leaf curl.

Some Hints on Saving Seeds

There is no doubt that properly grown bio-dynamic seeds are superior to any which can be bought through the usual trade channels. Not only do they keep much longer, but from germination onwards plants derived from them are sturdier and healthier.

GENERAL PRINCIPLES

Use 500 before sowing.
Use 501 a when the crop is established;
        b just before flowering;
        c soon after the seed has set.
The last of these applications is the most important if all cannot be managed.

Get the original seed stock from a reliable seedsman or from an organic or bio-dynamic source known to be good. If the seed has been treated with an insecticide or a fungicide, wash it well before sowing. Do not use F^1 or F^2 hybrids (which will be stated on the packet); seed from these will not come true to type.

Choose varieties which are known to do well in your district.

Sow as early as possible in your area, using cloches if necessary. The British climate apart from East Anglia is by no means ideal for raising seed, but earlier sown crops experience to the full the out-flowing spring and summer forces. The newly formed seeds are then ready to receive the ripening stream coming from the sun when it stands in the constellation of the Lion from mid-August to mid-September.

If you are growing seed for the first time, start with something simple such as leeks or beans.

Try to keep the strain pure by:

    a not growing other varieties of the crop which will flower at the same time;

    b by pulling up weak plants before flowering;

    c by removing any plants which appear to have a differing leaf or flower form.

Harvest during a waning moon unless conditions are exceptionally favourable during a waxing period.

Dry the seed pods very thoroughly by spreading them out on newspaper or hessian in a greenhouse or warm shed. Seed-bearing stems can be hung up to dry; enclose them in large paper bags perforated at the top if the seed is likely to shatter.

Clean the seed well by:

    a using a series of graded sieves;

or b gently blowing off the chaff and light seeds;

or c winnowing in the wind or in front of a fan;

or d letting them roll down a gently shaken inclined tray; the chaff and rubbish will stay at the top and the seed will collect at the bottom.

Store the seeds in air-tight containers—tins, screw-top jars, etc. Small seeds are best put into envelopes first.

The 'shelf life' of seeds varies greatly according to species. Parsnips are probably the worst, but bio-dynamic parsnip seed will still germinate up to 60 per cent after two years' storage. Most of the pea and bean family will keep for four or five years, and brassicas are often good for up to ten years.

The following detailed hints all relate to vegetables, but the same general principles apply to flowers.

Brassicas

These all intercross very easily, and it is difficult to ensure that cross pollination does not occur because the bees and flies which visit the flowers have already been to other kinds of brassicas in the neighbourhood and are carrying pollen from them. The professional seedsman or plant breeder puts a bag over each mother plant just before the flowers start to open and inserts some fly maggots such as are used by fishermen for bait; the flies act as pollinators when they hatch. The bags are made from a material which admits air but keeps out rain. These are the ideal requirements unlikely to be attained by a home gardener, but it is quite possible to improvise on similar lines.

Nearly all kinds of brassicas come into flower in May-June and ripen their seed at the ideal time. One or two typical plants of the variety from which seeds are required can be left to flower in their original positions; they must be bagged on the lines described. When the first pods have turned quite brown they are nearly ready to burst open and shed the seeds, so the whole plant is cut at ground level and hung up to dry out fully upside down with the bag still on. Threshing the unburst pods and collecting the seed from the bag can be done later in the year.

French Beans (Dwarf)

It is best to grow a few plants especially for seed. Start them under cloches or in pots in a greenhouse. When they come into flower support them with strings, twigs or wires so that the pods do not touch the ground. The plants should be widely spaced; if too close, moulds may develop on the young pods in damp weather. Pick the first pods when they have turned colour and started to shrivel and put them in a suitable place to dry out completely. Later, pull up the whole plants and hang them up to dry leaving plenty of room between them. Thresh when convenient, but it is a good plan to put all the pods on the top of a stove for an hour or two to make the sheaths thoroughly brittle.

Leeks

Select a few of the best plants in the over-wintered main plot and leave them to come into flower in June. One plant only will give sufficient seed to last a small garden for at least two seasons. Tie the flowering stems to stakes. When the stems begin to turn yellow, cut them about 30 cm (1 ft) below the seed head and hang up to dry before threshing. It is better not to take seed from a plant which has bolted early as this tendency may be transmitted to its offspring.

Lettuce

Leave a few of the best plants to run to seed, but only from early sowings or over-wintered plants. Alternatively one can transplant some seedlings to a place of their own for seeding so that they will not get in the way by occupying space needed for other crops. It takes a surprisingly long time for such a quick crop to mature its seed, and sowings from mid-May onwards will not mature properly in most seasons. When the first seed heads become fluffy and ready to blow away, cut the whole stems and put to dry with the usual precautions against shattered seeds.

Marrows

Under this heading are included pupkins, squashes, courgettes and melons. The first three all intercross easily, so it is necessary in the evening to fix a small paper bag over a female flower which is clearly ready to open the next morning. (Female flowers are easily recognised by the bulb at the base of the flower.) In the morning take an opening male flower from the same or a similar plant, strip off the corolla and put the remaining parts into the opening female: then replace the bag for a day or two. Mark carefully the fruit which develops and leave it on the plant until it dies back in the autumn. Store the fruit in a dry place and cut open during the winter. Rub the seeds out from the pulp, discarding those which are not plump and well shaped, wash if necessary and allow to dry thoroughly before storing. Melon seed, however, can be taken when the fruit is eaten; it is cleaned in the same way as described for tomatoes (see p. 196). All these seeds are quite long-lived and will remain viable for at least five years. In this category it is important to note that zucchinis nowadays are nearly always F^1 hybrids and seed from them if it sets at all is worthless.

Parsley

Treat as for carrots (under root crops), but there is no need to dig up and replant. The same holds good for caraway.

Peas

Reserve a portion of the first sown row for seed and do not grow another variety which will come into flower at the same time. Use the later pods for the table. Cut the whole plants at ground level when the earliest pods look like splitting open. Spread them out on sacking or hang them up in bags until the tops are quite dry. Thresh when convenient.

Radishes

Leave a few good specimens, true to their type, from the first outdoor sowing of the year, allowing at least a foot between them. Watch out for bird damage and net if necessary; greenfinches relish the half-ripe seed. Allow the plant to die back, cut and hang up for final drying. Strip the pods from the stems before threshing, There is little danger of shattering; in fact the pods are often tough and difficult to break open unless they are tinder dry.

Root Crops

Most of our root crops are biennials—that is, in the year of sowing they form a root as a storage organ to provide nourishment for flowering and seeding in the following year. Beetroot, onions, swedes, turnips, black radish, kohl rabi, celeriac, parsnips, Hamburg parsley and carrots all come into this category; the last four belong to the Umbelliferae family. The general principle for obtaining seed from all these is to select a few good specimens from the winter stores and to replant them early in the new year as soon as conditions permit. Plant them in good soil (treated with 500) 45–60 cm (18–24 in) apart with their tops just below the soil surface. Most of them will require staking when they come into flower. Cut the whole stems and put them to dry off when the first seeds are ripe and perhaps beginning to shatter.

The Umbelliferae need rather different treatment because they usually produce a 'king head' followed by a number of side shoots. The seed on the former ripens early and will start to shatter even before some of the side shoots have come into flower. Watch carefully for the first signs of shedding, cut the heads with their stems and put to dry in bags or between sheets of newspaper so that the shed seed is not lost. About a fortnight later cut the next heads as they ripen, and finally cut the whole plants. Sometimes the very last shoots will only produce small seeds which are not worth harvesting.

Do not save seed from any of these root crop plants which flower ('bolt') during the year of sowing; this undesirable tendency might be inherited in the next generation.

Scarlet Runners (and other climbing beans)

Leave two of the best beans on the first three bunches, using any more on the bunches for eating. Do not pick the pods until they have turned quite brown and then dry them off further on trays. Seed from later beans seldom fills out well and its development may be checked by an early frost.

Tomatoes

Choose well developed shapely fruit on the second or third truss and allow to ripen fully (even to split) before picking. Do not choose a fruit with green shoulders. Separate the seed from the pulp with your fingers. Rub off as much of the mucilage as possible in several washings of water, or rub the seed against the mesh of a fine sieve under a slowly running tap. Some people prefer to do the first rubbing in wood ashes or very fine sand which can then be easily washed off. Finally rub in a dry cloth and spread the seed on a sheet of glass or paper to dry off fully before storing in envelopes. For those who only grow a dozen plants or less the seed from one fruit will be sufficient to supply several years' needs.

CONCLUSION

Saving seed can be an interesting and profitable hobby, but the job must be done thoroughly and properly. Only the bare outlines have been given here. Saving poor seed is a waste of time and may cause great disappointment both to the saver and possibly to his or her friends. Seed for sowing should not be harvested on a 'root' day. According to Maria Thun it is more liable to fungal disease.

Resource List

1. Seeds

A growing range of biodynamically grown and Demeter registered vegetable, flower and herb seeds is now available in the UK by mail order. Many of these varieties have been grown on biodynamic holdings in the UK while others are imported from Germany, Switzerland, and Holland where biodynamic plant breeding and seed production has been established for many years.

The Biodynamic Agricultural Association is currently seeking to establish a wider network of farmers and gardeners across the UK willing to help supply the growing market for organic seeds with high quality biodynamically maintained varieties. Ongoing involvement and participation in a programme of biodynamic plant breeding is also encouraged. As a key project being promoted by the Biodynamic Agricultural Association any donations towards supporting its development are extremely welcome.

Hybrid varieties though seemingly uniform and productive have been shown to be deficient in terms of mineral content, flavour, keeping quality and digestibility. Such seeds will not breed true and so are also unsuited for home saving. Since hybrids were primarily introduced as a means for protecting breeder's rights, they are not necessarily better than well maintained non-hybrids. All the biodynamic seeds being developed and offered for sale are therefore non-hybrid open pollinated varieties.

A wide and increasing range of biodynamically grown vegetable, herb and flower seeds are now available by mail order. To obtain the annually produced catalogue contact: **Stormy Hall Seeds, Bottom Village, Danby, Whitby, N Yorks, YO21 2NJ**.

A large collection of biodynamically grown herb plants and seeds are also available from: **Poyntzfield Herb Nursery, Black Isle, by Dingwall, Ross & Cromarty, IV7 8LX**.

2. Biodynamic Preparations

Ready made Biodynamic Preparations, Preparation making materials and other specialist supplies are available from: **Biodynamic Supplies, Lorieneen, Bridge of Muchalls, Stonehaven, Aberdeen, AB39 3RU**.

3. Books

A wide range of books on biodynamic gardening, farming and related subjects are available by mail order from the **Biodynamic Agricultural Association, Painswick Inn Project, Gloucester Street, Stroud, GL5 1QG** (see Appendix C).

4. Contacts across the world

Australia
Biodynamic Farming & Gardening Assoc. In Australia Inc, P.O. Box 54, Bellingen, N.S.W. Australia 2454.
Tel: ++61-266-55 05 66 Fax: -55 85 51
Email: poss@midcoast.com.au

Brazil
ABD – Associacao Brasileria de Agricultura Biodinamica, Alexandre Harkaly, Sergio Pimenta, Caixa, Postal 321, 18603-970 Botucatu /SP Brazil.
Tel/Fax: 0055 14 6821 7862
Email: abd@abd.com.br
www.Abd.com.br

Canada
Society for Biodynamic Farming & Gardening in Ontario, R.R. #4 Bright Ontario NOJ 1BO
Tel/Fax: (519) 684-6846

Egypt

Egyptian Biodynamic Association, Heliopolis, El Horreya, P.O. Box 2834, Cairo, Egypt.
Tel: + 20 2280 79 94   Fax: + 20 2280 69 59
Email: ebda@sekim.com

France

Movement de Culture Biodynamique, 5, Place de la Gare, Colmar, F-68000, France.
Tel: + 33 389 24 36 41   Fax: + 33 389 24 27 41
Email: Biodynamis@wanadoo.fr

Germany

Forschungsring für Biologisch-Dynamische Wirtschaftsweise e. V., Brandschneise 2, D-64295, Darmstadt.
Tel: 49 6155 841241   Fax: 49 84 69 11

Holland

Vereniging voor Biologisch Dynamische Landbouw, Postbus 17, Diederichslaan 25 NL-3970 AA Driebergen.
Tel: 0031-34 35-3 17 40   Fax: 0031 3435 16943
Email: bd.vereniging@ecomarkt.nl
Email: kraayhof@worldaccess.nl

India

Biodynamic Agriculture Association of India, No 78 1st Floor, 11th Cross, Indiranager 1st Stage, IND-Bangalore 560 038.
Tel: 0091 33225 001564   Fax: 0091 33225 9511

Ireland

Biodynamic Agricultural Association in Ireland, The Watergarden, Thomastown, Co. Kilkenny, Ireland.
Tel: + 353 565 4214   Fax: + 353 508 73424

Italy

Assoziazione per l'Agricultura Biodinamica, Via Vasto 4, I-20121, Milano.
Tel: + 39 02 2900 2544   Fax: + 39 02 2900 0692

New Zealand

The Biodynamic Farming and Gardening Association in N.Z. Inc, P.O. Box 39045, Wellington Mail Centre, N.Z.
Tel: + 64 4 589 5366   Fax: + 64 4 589 5365
Email: biodynamics@clear.net.nz

South Africa
The Biodynamic Association of Southern Africa, P.O. Box 115, Paulshof ZA-2056.
Tel: + 27 118 0371 91   Fax: + 27 118 0371 91

Sweden
Biodynmiska Föreningen, Skillebyholm, S-15391, Järna, Sweden.
Tel: + 46 8551 51225   Fax: + 46 8551 51227

Switzerland
Landwirtschafliche Abteilung am Goetheanum, Hügelweg 59, CH-4143, Dornach.
Tel: + 41 61 706 4212   Fax: + 41 61 7061 42 15
Email: landw.abteilung@goetheanum.ch

USA
Biodynamic Farming and Gardening Association Inc; Building 1002B, Thoreau Center, The Presido, P.O. Box 29135, San Francisco, CA 94129 – 0135.
Tel: + 880 561 7797   Fax: + 880 561 7796
Email: biodynamics@aol.com
www.biodynamics.com

APPENDIX C

Bibliography and References

Recommended supplementary reading for gardeners

Agriculture – R. Steiner
Translated and edited by Catherine Creeger and Malcolm Gardner
With this remarkable series of lectures, Rudolf Steiner founded bio-dynamic agriculture. They contain profound insights into farming, the plant and animal world, the nature of organic chemistry and the influences of heavenly bodies. Published by the Biodynamic Farming and Gardening Association Inc. (USA) 1993. 310pp.

Biodynamic Gardening – some hints – K. Castelliz
A short booklet with very practical hints by a life-long practitioner. Published by the Biodynamic Agricultural Association.

Biodynamic Greenhouse Management – H. Grotzke
Full of practical tips on soil blends, light, sanitation and cuttings. Published by the Biodynamic Farming and Gardening Association Inc. (USA) 1988.

Biodynamic Sprays – H. Koepf
This introductory booklet describes how the biodynamic sprays are made, how they influence cultivation, and how they are to be used. It is a good reference for anyone working with the biodynamic sprays and preparations. Published by the Biodynamic Farming and Gardening Association Inc. (USA).

The Biodynamic Treatment of Fruit Trees – E. Pfeiffer
Basic principles and practical guidance on growing top and soft fruit. Describes measures to take in order to develop a pest-free orchard without the use of chemicals. Published by the Biodynamic Farming and Gardening Association Inc. (USA).

Companion Plants and How to Use Them – H. Philbrick and R. Gregg
An essential guide for gardeners wishing to make use of the beneficial and avoiding harmful plant combinations. Published by The Devon Adair Company, Old Greenwich, Conn. (USA) 1991.

Culture and Horticulture – W. Storl
Layman and gardener alike will thoroughly enjoy this book and benefit from a deeper philosophical and practical understanding of horticulture. An excellent introduction to biodynamics. Published by Biodynamic Farming and Gardening Association Inc. (USA).

The Ever Changing Garden – A. Klingborg
A history of garden design from a biodynamic perspective, filled with beautiful paintings and drawings. Published by the Lanthorn Press 1988.

Gardening for Health & Nutrition – J. & H. Philbrick
A detailed introduction to biodynamic gardening by the author of Companion Plants. Published by Anthroposophic Press (USA) 1988.

Gardening for Life – Maria Thun
A practical introduction to a holistic approach to biodynamic gardening, sowing, planting and harvesting written by Maria Thun, a well-known gardener and author of biodynamic techniques. Published by Hawthorn Press 1999.

Grow a Garden and be Self-Sufficient – E. Pfeiffer and E. Riese
The 'classic' introduction to biodynamic gardening by Ehrenfried Pfeiffer who for many years was the driving force behind biodynamics in the U.S. This book is full of practical suggestions which are as relevant today as when it was first published during the war. Published by Mercury Press (USA) 1999.

Handbook on Composting and the Preparations – G. Corrin
A basic introduction to biodynamic composting for farm and garden. Published by the Biodynamic Agricultural Association 1999.

Life to the Land – Guidelines for biodynamic husbandry – K. Castellitz
Filled with experiences gleaned from a life-times work with the
Preparations. Published by Lanthorn Press 1999.

**Organic Growing Media, Research into the use of compost for potting
mix nutrition** – W. Brinton & D. Tresemer
Published by Woods End Laboratory (USA) 1988.

Stella Natura – S. Wildfeurer
A sowing and planting calendar published annually in the USA, filled
with fascinating articles on biodynamics. Published by Biodynamic
Farming and Gardening Association Inc. (USA).

Studying the Agriculture Course – J. Soper
Notes and experiences gained through many years of working with the
lectures. Published by Biodynamic Agricultural Association. 1991.

Weeds and What They Tell – E. Pfeiffer
This booklet presents one small segment of Pfeiffer's knowledge of
living plants: how they grow, what they reveal about their surroundings and how their powers may be harvested for the benefit of those
who can appreciate and use them. Published by Biodynamic Farming
and Gardening Association Inc. (USA).

Working with the Stars – A Biodynamic Sowing and Planting Calendar
– M. Thun
The well known calendar published annually by Floris Books.

All the above books along with further titles are available from the
**Biodynamic Agricultural Association, Painswick Inn Project,
Gloucester Street, Stroud, Glos, GL5 1QG. Tel: 01453 759501. Email:
bdaa@biodynamic.freeserve.co.uk**

The Biodynamic Agricultural Association

The primary object of the Association is to foster and promote the agricultural impulse started by Rudolf Steiner in 1924 when he gave his course of eight lectures on agriculture. A close connection is kept with other aspects of Steiner's work, especially that of nutrition, social reform and natural science. Links are also maintained with other organisations concerned with organic farming and gardening, with the environment and with wider issues of sustainability today.

Membership of the Association is open to anyone interested in this work and is not confined to those practically engaged in farming and gardening.

The Association publishes a journal, *Star and Furrow*, twice a year in summer and winter (this is free to members); it contains articles both of a philosophical and practical nature, accounts of conferences and meetings, book reviews, correspondence from members and notes of work being carried out in other countries. It also covers subjects related to agriculture including nutrition.

A regular member's newsheet is issued, usually four times a year; it deals mainly with Association news, forthcoming events, practical hints and topics of general interest.

At least one national or international conference is arranged each year. Regional conferences, workshops and other events are arranged from time to time.

Groups exist in various areas of the United Kingdom for the

purposes of study, discussion and the practical application of the methods recommended.

There is a reference library for the benefit of members which comprises a wide range of publications covering the whole field of organic and biodynamic husbandry. Details are available on request.

The Association also owns and administers the Demeter Certification Trademark which is used by biodynamic producers to guarantee compliance with internationally recognised biodynamic production standards. Demeter is recognised by the UK Registry of Organic Foods Standards (UKROFS) as Organic Certification (UK 6).

Further information about the Association, its activity and all aspects of biodynamic farming and gardening can be obtained from:

Biodynamic Agricultural Association (BDAA)
Painswick Inn Project
Gloucester Street
Stroud
Glos
GL5 1QG
Tel/Fax: 0845 345 8474 (local rate) or 01453 759501
Email: bdaa@biodynamic.freeserve.co.uk
Or visit our website: www.anth.org.uk/biodynamic

Index